EARLY CHILDHOOD THEORIES

Today

EARLY CHILDHOOD THEORIES

Today

AARON BRADBURY
RUTH SWAILES

Learning Matters

A SAGE Publishing Company
1 Oliver's Yard
55 City Road
London EC1Y 1SP

SAGE Publications Inc.
2455 Teller Road
Thousand Oaks, California 91320

SAGE Publications India Pvt Ltd
B 1/I 1 Mohan Cooperative Industrial Area
Mathura Road
New Delhi 110 044

SAGE Publications Asia-Pacific Pte Ltd
3 Church Street
#10-04 Samsung Hub
Singapore 049483

Library of Congress Control Number: 2022933353

British Library Cataloguing in Publication Data

A catalogue record for this book is available from the British Library

Editor: Amy Thornton
Senior project editor: Chris Marke
Project management: TNQ Technologies
Marketing manager: Lorna Patkai
Cover design: Wendy Scott
Typeset by: TNQ Technologies
Printed in the UK

ISBN: 978-1-5297-9122-8
ISBN: 978-1-5297-9121-1 (pbk)

At SAGE we take sustainability seriously. Most of our products are printed in the UK using FSC papers and boards. When we print overseas we ensure sustainable papers are used as measured by the PREPS grading system. We undertake an annual audit to monitor our sustainability.

CONTENTS

DEDICATION AND ACKNOWLEDGEMENTS

Peter Swailes

This book is dedicated to Peter Swailes

Pete was a primary school teacher for almost 30 years, having started his career as a glassmaker and artist.

I first met Pete in 1988 and we started going out a few months later. He'd come to my home town of Chesterfield for work following a summer spent working in New York making glass, after completing his degree in 3D design. In 1990 due to a restructure, Pete was made redundant. Jobs were scarce at that time and Pete took to volunteering at Grassmoor primary school alongside some casual work as a part-time lecturer in the arts. He enjoyed working with children so much that he decided to study for a PGCE, and in 1992 landed his first teaching job, a temporary one-year contract, in the school I attended as a child. Under the guidance of Josie Fisher, an experienced, creative headteacher with a love of all things artistic, Pete flourished and became a permanent member of staff, staying at the school for 22 years.

Under Josie's leadership, Pete was encouraged to introduce creativity and the arts into the classroom, and he was well known among teachers and pupils alike for his sense of humour, his creative flair, his legendary untidy desk, his ability to knock up a piece of scenery in minutes and his talent for finding something that made every child tick. As **DT** lead he was involved in exciting projects working with industry leaders and was involved in contributing to the building schools for the future programme with the Local Authority, before the funding was removed by the new education secretary, Michael Gove. Former pupils and colleagues speak of Pete fondly, remembering projects, trips to Yorkshire Sculpture Park and the Hockney Gallery in Saltaire, his involvement for many years with the 'Take one Picture' project at Chatsworth House and his kindness both as a colleague and teacher.

When Josie retired, the school merged to become a primary school and Pete ventured into the juniors, which allowed him to explore more challenging creative projects. It was around this time that I purchased some studio time for Pete as a Christmas present. He hadn't had much opportunity to pursue his art and creative side outside of work as the demands of school life and parenting were heavy. I thought he might enjoy working with ceramics, something he hadn't done since he was a student at WR Tuson College, Preston, in 1982.

In 2014, when I decided to become a full-time advisor, Pete took the decision to leave full-time teaching. With me on the road a lot, someone needed to be around to support our two children who were 7 and 12 at the time and he felt that this wasn't possible with a full-time teaching commitment. Peter Swailes Ceramics was born, initially at home, and Pete supplemented our income with supply teaching in a couple of schools, always fitting work around family life. He was able to be at concerts, open days, parents' evenings and to pick the children up from school, something that just hadn't been possible when we were both teaching full-time. Over the next few years, the business began to grow, Peter moved into West Studios on Sheffield Road in 2015 and began teaching evening classes at Chesterfield College and reduced his teaching commitment to working with just one school, Abercrombie Primary in Chesterfield, a few minutes' walk from his studio.

Tracy Gannon, Headteacher at Abercrombie, had worked with Pete for a number of years when she was Deputy Head at his previous school and recognised his skills and talents as an artist and teacher. Pete was always willing to work with any class, from Nursery to Year 6, often at the drop of a hat, sometimes popping in for an hour, covered in clay when cover was needed. He was a well-liked member of the school team, by staff, pupils and parents. Working at Abercrombie gave Pete back his love of teaching, his favourite place was always in the classroom and he was never a fan of paperwork, so to get back to what he loved, being with the children without the pressures of excessive bureaucracy, gave him a great deal of joy. He would often help out voluntarily at events at the school and attended staff training. He really enjoyed being part of the Abercrombie team. At the other end of the spectrum, Pete was enjoying teaching adults and post 16 students' ceramics skills. It really felt like everything was coming together.

When COVID hit in March 2020, our lives were turned upside down; I couldn't go into schools and Pete couldn't go into the studio, so he started to make things at home. The kitchen table became his studio and we built a small kiln shed in the garden. It was a pleasure and a blessing to be able to spend so much time together at home. Pete's work became increasingly popular, and 2020 was his most successful year as a potter. Throughout 2020, we often talked about how hard lockdown must be for people living with an illness, knowing that your time was limited, which seems strangely prescient now.

In early 2021, Pete started to have stomach pains, and when he sneezed or coughed it was extremely painful. After many telephonic consultations and two visits to the hospital, we were told that Pete had terminal cancer, which had already spread from his pancreas to his stomach and peritoneum, hence the excruciating pain. The specialist said he had months left to live.

That kind of news leaves you reeling. But the time following diagnosis gave us a lot of opportunity to reflect. Many people told us how Pete has made a difference to their lives, former pupils and parents of former pupils have been in touch and told us what a difference Pete made when he taught them. Colleagues have taken the time to write to me about his kindness and generosity and his obvious care for the children he worked with. Customers speak of how his work has given them great joy, and complete strangers got in touch via social media to tell him how inspired they were by the way he dealt with his illness. The last few months of Pete's life, though tinged with sadness, were also filled with joy and love.

The one positive of a terminal diagnosis is that people are able to tell the person how they feel about them. What was overwhelming was just how many people got in touch to tell us what a difference Pete made to their lives. Everyone mentioned his creativity. One of the things which frustrated him most about working in school towards the end of his full-time teaching career was the increasing pursuit of uniformity. The expectation that every class, regardless of their makeup and age range, was expected to work in the same way. This led to Pete feeling stifled and frustrated and probably contributed to him being more inclined to leave full-time teaching than he would otherwise have been. It seemed to matter more that his work was marked using a purple pen, rather than whether the children were engaged in their learning and making progress. The thing which had been his strength, his ability to be responsive and creative, was viewed by those who mistake consistency for uniformity as his greatest flaw. Consistency is about quality and reliability rather than everyone being and doing the same. In every school we need a range of teachers, who will share their joys, passions and skills with the pupils they teach. We need a consistent curriculum, but the how, the way that this is delivered, should vary year on year, depending on the children being taught, responding to their uniqueness. This is very much an underlying principle of the Early Years Foundation Stage (EYFS), and one which Pete held dear to his heart. No scheme or unit of work has met the children in the classroom, and the skill of the teacher is to respond to their uniqueness and build their knowledge and skills. Otherwise, we become mere deliverers of content, when teaching is so much more than that. I am so glad that Pete got the opportunity to teach like that again at Abercrombie.

Aaron and I had already agreed to edit this book before we knew Pete was ill. After his diagnosis, when Aaron suggested dedicating the book to Pete, Pete was somewhat overcome. I think it is a perfect opportunity to reflect on the kind of teachers we want to see in our classrooms. Some things need to be consistent: expectations, relationships, nurture and support. But there must always be space in the classroom for the individuals who form part of the community. The unique child and their unique teachers. For spontaneity and creativity. Hopefully you will find plenty in the pages that follow to inspire you and to reflect on the kind of practitioner you want to be and to consider how the children in your care see you.

It is telling that more often than not, Pete's former pupils mention memories of creative projects, of the way something was taught to engage and spark interest, of the moments when the opportunity arose and was seized rather than sticking rigidly to the script. That's a legacy to be proud of.

We also want to say thank you to all of the contributors of this book and the editing team at Sage. It has been a pleasure working with you all, and here is to the next one.

We both have had a great time writing together and have developed a friendship which will continue to last and enhance our Early Childhood pedagogies into the future.

Peace, Joy and Love to you all.

Aaron and Ruth

ABOUT THE EDITORS

Aaron Bradbury is an Early Childhood academic, paying close attention to all aspects of Early Years and child-centred practice, workforce development, child development and Early Help. His current role is Principal Lecturer for Early Years and Childhood at Nottingham Trent University. He is also the Chair of the LGBTQ Early Years working group and manages his own website and community called Early Years Reviews. He has published texts on apprenticeships and Early Years research.

Ruth Swailes has more than 25 years' experience in primary education, over 20 of them in senior leadership roles including primary headship. Ruth has worked as a School Improvement Advisor, Early Years consultant and moderator in several Local Authorities, supporting leaders and teachers to improve outcomes for pupils. Passionate about primary education, particularly Early Years, Ruth has taught from Nursery to Year 6.

ABOUT THE AUTHORS

Kate Irvine is a Foundation Years Consultant for a local authority and a governor of a maintained nursery school with over 20 years of experience in the birth to five sector, nurseries, children's centres and primary education. She is a qualified teacher and has a masters in educational practice with specialist knowledge in the Early Years. Kate is particularly interested in assessment and transition, literacy and the reception year of the EYFS, and is currently developing an academic research project into supporting transitions into year one.

Meredith Rose is a Senior Lecturer and Course Leader (Early Years) at Nottingham Trent University. Meredith has an industry background in the Early Years in both the private and maintained sector and managed a day nursery. Meredith progressed into training and onto teaching in Further Education for over 10 years. In 2018, Meredith began at Nottingham Trent University and is now a lead for a special interest group (SIG) in Early Childhood which focuses on current agendas and debates within the sector. Her research interests include leadership, the value and recognition of play within our society, and the curricula for Early Childhood degrees.

Pam Jarvis is a chartered psychologist, historian, researcher and grandparent. She received her PhD from Leeds Beckett University in 2005 for her thesis on the narratives children create in spontaneous rough and tumble play. She retired from lecturing in 2019, and is now a journalist and author. She writes articles, books and chapters relating to theory and practice in education and Early Years, including the bestsellers *Perspectives on Play* and *Early Years Pioneers*, and contributes to staff training initiatives. She has recently published her first novel.

Philippa Thompson is Principal Lecturer in Early Childhood Studies at Sheffield Hallam University and Co-Chair of the Early Childhood Studies Degrees Network (ECSDN). Her research interests in Early Childhood include play, participation, outdoor learning and parents and children living with anaphylaxis. Previous roles have included a local authority advisory teacher for Early Years, head of nursery/foundation stage in a range of settings and an outdoor education leader in Australia. Philippa has written on a variety of issues relevant to Early Childhood students and practitioners and is mum to Tom aged 16 years who is forever helping her to think and learn.

Sue Allingham is an independent consultant, author and trainer. Her expertise and passion for teaching and learning in the Early Years started with her classroom experience and senior lead role as Early Years co-ordinator in the late 1980s. Sue gained an MA followed by a doctorate, both in Early Years education from Sheffield University. Her solid grounding in research informs her training and consultancy as well as the articles she writes for the *Early Years Educator* magazine as a Consultant Editor.

Tamsin Grimmer is an experienced Early Years consultant, author and lecturer. She is the Early Years Director of Linden Learning and passionate about how young children learn. She believes that all children deserve practitioners who are inspiring, dynamic, reflective and loving. Tamsin particularly enjoys delivering training and supporting Early Childhood educators to improve outcomes for young children.

Valerie Daniel is a qualified teacher with over 30 years' experience with the last 13 years as a Maintained Nursery School headteacher. Her other roles include being a trustee for the Birmingham Nursery Schools Collaboration Trust (BNSCT) currently the chair of the Trust as well as sitting on a number of Local Authority Strategic groups. Valerie is one of 15 Birmingham Association of Maintained Nursery Schools (BAMNS) headteachers who work within a contractual collaboration. Valerie has a deep interest in the dynamics of the current Early Years Sector and received her Doctorate in Education from the University of Birmingham on her thesis titled 'The Perceptions of a Leadership Crisis in the Early Years Sector (EYS)'. She is also a trained Systems Leader and Leadership Mentor for other headteachers and leaders in the Early Years Sector.

INTRODUCTION

Early Childhood pioneers and theorists are the backbone of our practices in working with children 0–8 years and families. We continually hear about how we need to link theory to practice as it allows us to continue to put the child at the centre of what we do. The Early Childhood pioneers and theorists undoubtedly influence our thinking when it comes to child development and our practices.

This book engages the reader, that's you by the way, in thought-provoking practices when it comes to Early Childhood. Yes, of course we have some of the names we have come to love and respect, the greats, the ones we were all taught when we did our training, but this book also highlights some of what we class as modern-day theorists or pioneers. It is of course these professionals that are supporting the landscape, our thinking and critical eyes when it comes to us being with children and families. We both think that you will enjoy the full range of theorists and pioneers with a contemporary twist. We have chosen these theorists and pioneers as not only do we feel that these have made huge gains in the sector, but we also still believe that they are influencing our practices today and hope that they will influence yours into the future too.

AIMS OF THE BOOK

The main aim of this book is to support your journey as an Early Childhood professional, practitioner, or student doing training in the field of Early Years, Early Primary Education, Early Childhood and Community role. It is a text which supports you to demonstrate how to apply your knowledge and understanding to Early Childhood in a holistic way. The book will also go a long way to supporting you with applying theory to practice. Working across a range of Early Childhood practices we know how daunting or confusing it can be with the wide range of theorists and pioneers out there and determining which is the best one for approaching certain aspects of your practice. We can safely say that no matter which theorist you use from this text, whether that is a modern-day one or one from the past, we have chosen them for their child-centred approach to Early Childhood practices, so their concepts meet many aspects of being an Early Childhood professional today and what is needed to be a 21st century professional. This book has been written at a time when children's learning is being impacted in many ways due to the Coronavirus (COVID-19) pandemic. However, we are clear that children need us to be able to see the world through their eyes, and by giving you our 10 Early Childhood theorists and Pioneers, we hope, in some way help us to support and guide each child to be able to fulfil their childhood and develop into joyous, unique and well-supported individuals.

ABOUT THIS BOOK

The book is divided into 10 chapters, with the importance of love, child-centred practice and pedagogical approaches in children's learning and everyday lives at the centre. The book allows you to see those common threads running throughout the text. The book is also unique, as we feel that professionals in Early Childhood need to see how modern-day pioneers of Early Childhood are helping shape our landscape of practice today.

The chapters contain a range key features to help support your learning, such as chapter objectives, key definitions, reflective practice exercises, case studies, key questions and recommended further reading.

Each chapter focuses on either a modern-day theorist or pioneer, or one of the greats we have come to learn and love. The book has been written by several expert voices, depicting their ideas of how these theorists and pioneers link to Early Childhood practices. Each chapter gives you a detailed account of who the theorists and pioneers are and supports you with critical thinking, reflection and connection to your everyday practices. We wanted to share the expert author voices, making sure that the book was a representation of the workforce, and this has developed into the edited book you are now reading. We are very excited about this text, and we hope you enjoy reading it.

So, let's give a snippet of what is to come in the book by exploring each chapter.

BOOK CHAPTERS IN DETAIL

Chapter One – Stephen Bavolek

Chapter One is written by Aaron Bradbury and focuses on the work of Stephen Bavolek. It allows you to recognise the links being made in Early Childhood practice through the theory of Bavolek. It encompasses the role that empathy plays in Early Childhood practices and how to embed this to your role. Underpinning this is the approach of nurturing when working with children, parents, carers and the family.

Chapter Two – Urie Bronfenbrenner

Chapter Two is written by Tamsin Grimmer and focuses on the work of Urie Bronfenbrenner. Exploring the ecological systems theory is at the heart of this chapter, but it encompasses many modern-day explorations to Early Childhood practices, including how children do not grow up in isolation, the importance of looking at the context of a child's life and how a loving pedagogy can support a child's ecosystem.

Chapter Three – Pierre Bourdieu

Chapter Three is written by Kate Irvine and looks at a theorist we don't automatically recall when it comes to Early Childhood, Education and Care, Pierre Bourdieu. A theorist who is looked at during mostly within a post-graduate arena has now become mainstream for us all in this chapter. Kate writes about how his theory can support the theory of cultural capital, looking at how this is perceived today, exploring values and practices and how this affects provision for children and families. There are continual links that are made to establish Early Years approaches and theories within this chapter.

Chapter Four – Friedrich Froebel

Chapter Four is written by Meredith Rose and looks at the great work of Friedrich Froebel. The chapter looks at how you can use the theory and principles of Frobel in your practices today. You may get to the end of the chapter and realise that there are aspects of these that you can use in your own setting, alongside other established practices that already work for your children. Consider that theories and approaches can be used as a 'pick-n-mix counter', once you have a good understanding of them, as it is commonplace to see practitioners and settings using a blend of approaches as their practice which evolves in this chapter.

Chapter Five – Julie Fisher

Chapter Five is written by Ruth Swailes and looks at a modern-day theorist and pioneer Julie Fisher. The chapter recognises the links to Early Childhood practice through the theoretical perspectives of Julie Fisher. It considers the role of the practitioner starting from the perspective of the child in Early Childhood practice and moves onto the influence of transitions in education from Early Years to Key Stage One.

Chapter Six – Loris Malaguzzi

Chapter Six is written by Valerie Daniel and explores a contemporary twist of Loris Malaguzzi. This chapter gets you to recognise the links to Early Childhood practice through the theory of Loris Malaguzzi, learning and the rights of the child, valuing the environment as a third teacher and links to nurturing children is at the heart of this chapter.

Chapter Seven – Maria Montessori

Chapter Seven is written by Sue Allingham and looks at the work of Maria Montessori, depicting a contemporary discussion around practice and provision. The chapter will allow you to reflect on her theory in relation to current practices within an Early Childhood context. Working with children, parents and carers in the wider social context of the family is also explored in this chapter, giving it a current feel for your practice.

Chapter Eight – Tina Bruce

Chapter Eight is written by Philippa Thompson, looking at a modern-day theorist and pioneer Tina Bruce. This chapter allows you to recognise the links to Early Childhood practice through the theoretical perspectives of Tina Bruce. Playing close attention to the 12 features of play and the complexities of being able to define play. Links to other theory is made within the chapter, exploring the Froebelian Principles, further links to diversity and individuality and families are also explored. A modern-day pioneer with a contemporary twist to practice within Early Childhood.

Chapter Nine – Valerie Daniel

Chapter Nine is written by Aaron Bradbury exploring the work of Valerie Daniel. A modern-day pioneer in the Early Childhood sector. This chapter explores the rigour and knowledge of a powerful woman in the Early Years. A real focus on the work of Valerie Daniel and the learning which can take place from her work. The chapter focuses on three areas of her work, Leadership and Management in the Early Years, Anti-Racist and Anti-Oppressive practices and reclaiming safe spaces. A real eye-opener to seeking child-centred nurturing practices depicted through the eyes of a modern-day pioneer with the Early Childhood sector.

Chapter Ten – Margaret McMillan and Grace Owen

This chapter has been written by Pam Jarvis and takes a trip down memory lane. A history chapter exploring the work of Margaret McMillan and Grace Owen. Two well-respected pioneers within the field of Early Childhood. Watch out for the twist in this chapter though, depicting Nursery Wars during their time. A deeper look at debating and defining the modern nursery. Will you be able to see some of the similarities explored in this bonus chapter?

1

STEPHEN BAVOLEK

By Aaron Bradbury

CHAPTER OBJECTIVES

By the end of this chapter, you will be able to:

- Recognise the links to Early Childhood practice through the theory of Dr Bavolek.
- Define empathy and how this is embedded into Dr Bavolek's theory.
- Describe the nurturing practices of working with parents, carers and the wider family.
- Know how to apply nurturing care to enhance Early Childhood practice.
- Explain the importance of nurturing care for all children.

KEY DEFINITIONS

Nurturing	To take care of, feed, and protect someone or something, especially young children or plants, and help him, her, or it to develop.
Empathy	Is the ability to sense other people's emotions, coupled with the ability to imagine what someone else might be thinking or feeling.
Nurturing care	Refers to a stable environment created by parents and other caregivers that ensures children's good health and nutrition, protects them from threats and gives young children opportunities for early learning, through interactions that are emotionally supportive and responsive.
Emotional environment	Is one that promotes emotional well-being and provides stability for the children according to their individual needs. A good emotional environment will provide the children with: adults who will provide them with emotional support, understanding their feelings and showing empathy.

INTRODUCTION

It is important that we give credibility to some of the contemporary people who are leading the way within Early Childhood, and Dr Bavolek is no exception. You may not have heard of him as his work may not have been explored on training programmes. You may have focused on the more traditional theorists we have discussed elsewhere in this book. But, Dr Bavolek's research and theory really resonate with the child, the parent and the whole community, encompassing the concept of 'Nurturing' which his research is founded upon. His research is based around the premise of nurturing parents which was established in 1983. Dr Bavolek is a recognised leader in the field of working with children and young people of who have suffered neglect and abuse.

The research is growing that shows us that nurturing emotional relationships are the most primary function needed for both intellectual and social growth. Building on the well-established work of Bowlby (1979), Ainsworth (1978) and Robertson (with Bowlby, Robertson and Rosenbluth, 1952), authors, researchers and academics (some we explore elsewhere in this book), but also individuals such as Conkbayir (2017), Goswami (2006) and Zeedyk (2013), are using the science to help us explore the development of the human brain during the earliest years. At the most basic levels the science tells us that relationships which foster an element of warmth, intimacy and happiness form a strong sense of security for the child. This also builds on the work of Maslow (1970) who considers the need for physical safety, protection from injury and supplying basic needs for nutrition and housing/shelter. This mounting evidence shows how when there is a safe, secure, empathetic, and nurturing environment, children learn to be caring and empathetic. This eventually develops into becoming a reflective child, being able to link their own wishes, being able to communicate their own thoughts and feelings, and develop their own relationships.

Moving forwards to current times, the concepts of the nurturing approach are prevalent, not just with children who face adversities within their lives, but across the Early Childhood sector. This chapter will explore elements of Dr Bavolek's research and how we have interpreted it to support practice within Early Childhood. Nurturing and empathy, what these mean to the child, the professional and the family, and how to develop and maintain a secure relationship will be the focus of this chapter. We will explore how we can incorporate this into Early Childhood practice, and ultimately make conscious choices about how we as practitioners develop strong and secure attachments when it comes to adopting nurturing care approaches for the environment, the child and the family.

BIOGRAPHY

Stephen J. Bavolek is a recognised authority within the fields of child abuse and neglect, especially regarding treatment, prevention and parenting education. Stephen was born and raised in Chicago. His professional background includes working with the emotional needs of children and young people, including work within schools and residential settings. He worked extensively with abused children and abusive parents in treatment programmes.

Dr Bavolek has produced extensive research in the prevention and treatment of child and abuse and neglect. He received his doctorate at Utah State University in 1978, and he completed a post-doctorate at the Kempe Centre for the Prevention and Treatment of Child Abuse and Neglect in Denver, Colorado. He has worked in many universities including the University of

Wisconson – Eau Claire, and the University of Utah. In addition to his work, he has been selected by Oxfords Who's Who in 1993 as a member of the elite registry of extraordinary professionals. Since 1983, Dr Bavolek has conducted numerous workshops, been a voice on radio and television. He is the principal author of the 'Nurturing Parenting Programmes' (1983), which is designed to prevent and treat child abuse and neglect.

NURTURING

Nurturing is a word which is used very much within the fibres of Bavolek's work and research. Dr Bavolek's research fundamentally starts with the child and young person from a preventative model against Child Abuse and Neglect. However, there are certain points to consider from his research which relate to our own Early Childhood sector. We need to pay close attention to many factors within our own practice, encompassing the child and paying proximity to the environment where children are cared for, to support emotional well-being (Hunter et al., 2019). It is with this in mind that we wanted to explore some of the main outcomes of his research, but also how it could be used within our everyday practices.

In addition, Bavolek's research comes from the perspective of supporting parents to be 'nurturing parents'. It is with this in mind that we can take some of the aspects of his research and explore how this supports us as practitioners and professionals. For example, we can consider how we build on the relationships between the child and key care givers (or key person), and how we work and build relationships within our role advocating for children and young people.

NURTURING CARE

Bavolek's concept of 'Nurturing Care' consists of five interrelated components:

* health
* nutrition
* safety
* early learning
* responsive care

It is important that children are given all five domains of nurturing care to meet their developmental needs, and we will explore all of these in more detail a little later in the chapter. First, let's concentrate on the 'responsive care' component and the links to key relationships in a child's life.

In the first years of life, a warm, caring and responsive adult is best placed to support the nurturing care of a child. This could be as a parent, another family member, or as a professional. It is with this in mind that Bavolek supports that those relationships need to be built up with parents and carers, in order to support the child. In terms of our practice as professionals, this is where we can begin to see the importance of genuine partnerships with parents and family-centred approaches. We need to begin with the firm belief that all parents are interested in the development and progress of their own children. Parents want to be effective advocates on their children's behalf (Ball, 2004).

Bavolek promotes engagement between parents and the child as vital. Parents and carers often want to see, and delight in, some elements of responses to cuddling, eye contact, smiles, vocalisations and gestures even before any speech develops from the child. With the nurturing care approach, practitioners can support parents to see how through these mutually enjoyable interactions the child and parent are able to create a communication channel where the child is able to learn. Through these serve and return 'communications', very young children learn about the beginnings of language development, form cognitions and come to learn about the world around them. A nurturing care environment encourages the use of ongoing observation of the child (not necessarily formal), to learn about their needs and intentions. It is therefore important that professionals work with parents to support this notion, develop ideas and help to translate those observations in a way that describe and explain children's behaviours.

Child development pioneers, such as Erik Erikson, Anna Freud and Dorothy Burlingham, came to conclusions that to pass successfully through stages of early childhood, children require sensitive, nurturing care, which supports them being able to build capacities of trust, empathy and compassion. This is reassuring to those of us within the Early Childhood arena, particularly in how we teach, understand and embed empathy into our practice. This is an important link to Bavolek's research within the continuum of nurturing in its widest sense.

In effect, historical and contemporary research, such as discussed elsewhere in this book, shows us how supportive, warm, nurturing emotional interactions with young children help them to thrive, flourish, grow and develop. A range of science's now *prove* how this works. If we consider anatomy, for example, we now know *how* the nervous system links the brain and the body. There is a range of research on this subject, but a starting point could be some of the language, regarding how the nervous system fills every tiny space within the body, sending messages backwards and forwards at incredible speeds:

> … we can divide the nervous system into the *central nervous system* (CNS), consisting of the brain and the spinal cord and the *peripheral nervous system* (PNS) … [there is also] the *sympathetic system*, … and the *parasympathetic system*.

> (Brodal, 2004, p. xi)

Therefore, Bavolek fundamentally believes in this approach, having seen for himself, the effects of where/when children have not had a nurturing and safe environment. Sadly, this is a stark reality for some children, and we can now scientifically prove how this ultimately affects a child's nervous system, CNS and biology, and in turn, how this affects their life chances. While it must be acknowledged that there are still some debates, the discoveries that science is now sharing are unequivocal:

> A fundamental paradox exists and is unavoidable: development in the early years is both highly robust and highly vulnerable. Although there have been long-standing debates about how much the early years really matter in the larger scheme of lifelong development, our conclusion is unequivocal: What happens during *the first months and years of life* matters a lot, not because this period of development provides an indelible blueprint for adult well-being, but *because it sets either a sturdy or fragile stage for what follows*.

> (Shonkoff and Phillips, 2000, p. 5. emphasis added)

REFLECTIVE PRACTICE EXERCISE

Consider the following:

- How do babies learn to talk?
  - When do babies learn to talk?
  - Who helps babies learn to talk?
  - How do we help?
  - What do we do that helps?

And conversely – what do we do that does not always help?

For babies, listening to human voices helps them to learn and distinguish sounds and language. Therefore, it makes sense that a baby brought up in a 'sound-rich' environment will begin to imitate and copy the sounds around them. Likewise, consider how a baby growing up in an environment where there are warm and nurturing adults who respond to those sounds might feel, compared to a baby whose sounds are ignored? In other words, babies whose sounds are discouraged (or ignored) will learn something entirely different:

> The toddler who has learned that the people she depends on for comfort will help her when she is distressed is more likely to approach others with empathy and trust than the toddler whose worries and fears have been dismissed or belittled.
>
> (Shonkoff and Phillips, 2000, p. 90)

If this is the case with language (or sounds), we can take this further, and link to Dr Bavolek's work, and consider empathy.

EMPATHY

Empathy is the ability to recognise, understand and share the thoughts and feelings of another person, animal or even a toy, or fictional character. Developing empathy is something that supports us, as humans, in establishing relationships and being able to behave compassionately. Empathy involves being able to experience another person's point of view, rather than just being aware of our own. It enables what is known as 'helpful behaviours' or a 'pro-social' approach, which in turn supports friendships and acceptance. In other words, it is about behaviours that are coming from within a person, rather than being forced upon them.

The earlier discussions connect clearly to the theoretical application of Dr Bavolek when he considers empathy. He believes that empathy is fundamental to gaining and developing strong and secure relationships. Even though his research looks at this from the perspectives of a parent, the intention is that this ultimately links to, and is a benefit to, the child.

Before we delve into the depths of empathy, it is important to discuss what it looks and feels like. Empathy is a work in progress throughout childhood and into adolescence and is continually shaped by a range of factors including genetics, temperament, context, relationships and the environment. Empathy does not unfold automatically in children. While we are born hardwired with the capacity for empathy, its development requires experience and practice. Empathy is both an emotional and cognitive experience – and crucially it is different to sympathy.

Let's look at empathy in more detail.

Empathy comes from the Greek word 'empatheia' which means 'feeling into'. Let's break this down:

REFLECTIVE PRACTICE EXERCISE

Can you think of a time when you have seen a child showing empathy?
  Think when they showed empathy to another child, adult, pet or toy, for example?

• What happened?
• What types of feelings, behaviours and language were being shown by the child?
• Why do you think that?

Children can develop empathy, can't they?

It is shown within Dr Bavolek's research that he believes that empathy is the bedrock to supporting child and parent connections. So, let's explore how children develop empathy. Within children, empathy helps them cooperate with others around them, it allows them to build friendships and learn to make moral decisions, for example. You could also argue that this is an important aspect of lifelong development and that being able to further develop social and emotional skills, is vital to adults too:

Empathy, another ability that builds on emotional self-awareness, is the fundamental 'people skill'... the social cost of being emotionally-tone deaf, and the reasons empathy kindles altruism [unselfishness]. People who are empathetic are more attuned to the subtle social signals that indicate what others need or want.

(Goleman, 1996, p. 43)

Empathy is important as it helps us to connect with, and help others, but like many other traits, it may have evolved with a social antenna. What we mean here is the child looking and searching for the social aspects of other children, hence becoming the antenna. From an evolutionary perspective of children developing, being able to create a mental model of another person's intent is of critical interest. Children develop empathy, but children also need to be nurtured to be able to feel and understand what true empathy is.

EMOTIONAL COMPONENTS OF EMPATHY

Babies begin reflecting the emotional states and expressions of those around them almost from birth. As Zeedyk (2012) puts it, 'babies are born connected'. This is thanks to the Mirror Neuron System (MNS) which develops and strengthens as babies begin reflecting the emotional states and expressions of those around them. Infants as young as 18 hours old often show some responsiveness to other infants in distress. Likewise, if for example, you have ever stuck your tongue out at a very young baby, you will know exactly what happens. This is where the 'nature' vs 'nurture' debate used to come into play as we do not teach babies how to do this. You can find more detail on the great work by visiting the link below on how babies come into the world already connected to other people:

http://www.suzannezeedyk.com/wp-content/uploads/2016/03/Suzanne-Zeedyk-Babies-Connected-v2.pdf.

Science has now shown us that humans are born with a hardwired 'map' which in simple terms equates to their genetics, environmental factors and pre-birth experiences. In other words, being in a safe, supportive environment, with nurturing, supportive adults, from before birth, helps babies learn to perceive and respond to emotional cues. In turn, being able to exchange gestures (such as a smile), leads to babies and young children beginning to learn that they are different to us and can do different (or indeed the same) things. This is known as forming a sense of self.

These become the foundations of empathy, understanding that we can each experience different feelings and emotions. It is then easy to see why early emotional experiences between babies and their caregivers are crucial to the development of empathy. Bavolek's research on empathy, works on the links between emotional well-being and keeping empathy as a building block for being able to fulfil the relationship between child and caregiver. Within his research he fundamentally believes that developing skills of empathy can prevent child abuse and neglect through 'positive nurturing'.

Empathy has close links to emotional relationships and together these are believed to be the most crucial primary foundation for both intellectual and social growth. When children are part of secure, empathetic, nurturing relationships, in turn, children are then more able to be caring and empathetic. Ultimately the end result is the child being able to communicate their feelings, reflect on, and develop their own relationships. A nurturing relationship also teaches a child the behaviours which are appropriate and those which are not. You can see this within a two-year-old; a child's behaviours become more complex within their second of life, they start to learn from their care givers. Facial expressions, tone of voice, gestures, words and so on, all show the child what is approved and accepted and what is not. A pattern emerges which is built up through the give and take (or serve and return) interactions between children and caregivers. At this stage alongside these behaviours, the child is also starting to relate to their own internal emotions, and personal wishes and feelings are coming into being. These subtle emotional tones and interactions are vital to learn about who we are and what it is we want to do, or indeed, learn.

In addition, nurturing, as well as supporting emotional development, also supports cognitive development. Cognitive skills are about thinking, reasoning, imagining, wondering and so on – and again, science shows us that nurturing enables a child to learn to think. When a baby is born, their brain has almost all the neurons it will ever have, and by the age of two years, there is an increase of connections which are made (and later trimmed out) based on which ones are more frequently used. Therefore, a warm, nurturing environment supports connections and developments within the brain, while an adverse environment can harm development. If we link this to the previous discussions – does it make sense that if a child feels safe and supported, that they are more likely to be able to learn? and does it also then make sense, to consider how this relates to practice in Early Childhood?

WHAT IS NURTURING CARE IN EARLY CHILDHOOD PRACTICE?

Nurturing in the context of being a practitioner within the Early Childhood sector comes with an emphasis on the consistency of relationships. However, it can be that these consistent nurturing relationships that we have with children are often taken for granted for babies and young children. Practitioners do many of the nurturing outcomes without realising. Basically, it is about being in tune with the child. Being in tune means listening to and observing the child. Enabling the environment making care a complete child-centred approach. Making use of the parents and carers, advocating for the child. Let's look at how this can play out for the child in the case study below.

CASE STUDY

Rachel: An Early Years Professional.

Rachel has a positive relationship with her children in the preschool room, but she noticed that they struggled to settle after the weekend or holidays. Many children would display clinginess to their parents in the morning and would become anxious of leaving them. Rachel knew that much of the transition needed to happen before the children had even got the room. Rachel started to think about what needed to happen before the children even entered the nursery setting. Rachel thought about what it looks and feels like from the perspective of the child. So she started to change simple things in the entrance. Each child would leave something on a Friday and collect it again on the Monday. What Rachel needed to do was also see the setting from the child's eyes. So, she filmed a film with a go pro camera. Sent the family a video of Rachel welcoming back the child saying she is looking forward to seeing them.

REFLECTIVE QUESTIONS

- *Can you relate to the case study above? If so, how are you settling children into your nurturing environment?*
- *Have you been around your setting with a camera and seen it through the eyes of the child?*
- *How much emphasis do you put into applying child-centred transitions in your setting?*

If, as we have explored, nurturing, and the care that comes with this, is what a child needs, what the brain needs, and indeed depends upon for healthy development – how does this link to our practice? Let's look at this is in more detail.

ENABLING A NURTURING ENVIRONMENT

Bavolek considers how the nurturing environment plays a huge part of the child's development and emotional well-being. Again, this can be reassuring for those of us in the Early Childhood sector. The impact of the child's surroundings within their development is well documented in many pioneers of Early Childhood. Friedrich Froebel in the early (1800s) discusses an approach to designing an environment for children as an organic approach, an ever-changing garden, which can inspire and guide children's imagination and behaviour.

Similarly, this can be seen and mirrored in the Reggio Emilia approach as the environment is seen as a 'third teacher'.

HOW DO WE ENABLE A NURTURING ENVIRONMENT?

In order to enable a nurturing environment, it is essential that all professionals and practitioners understand how children thrive, flourish and learn, and the crucial value of play to support children in all aspects of their development. Nurturing can be seen through the key principle of observations. Through ongoing observations, we are able to learn not only what the child is learning but also how they are growing as individuals, and support their social and emotional developmental outcomes.

REFLECTIVE PRACTICE EXERCISE

Consider the children you work with:

- What outcomes would you expect to see from a nurturing environment?
  - From a baby's perspective?
  - From a young child's perspective?
  - From an older child's perspective?
  - From a parent's perspective?
  - From staff members' perspectives?
  - From a leaders/manager's perspective?

The above Reflective Practice exercise should help our thought process in creating nurturing environments for all. There are many positive outcomes of a nurturing environment, these are some, from children's perspectives, but we are sure you have come up with many more:

- Having an appropriate pace/rhythm to the day/session. Observing children shows us the importance of repetition, and where there is need for flexibility.
- Children are supported in the need to have the opportunities to explore, observe, take part and create their own experiences.

- The experiences offered focus on, and understand the importance of, the process rather than the product. This builds those nurturing opportunities, thought processes and strengthens the emotions when interacting with each other. It also supports observations on how children are processing the activity.
- Adult interruption of children's play is only when necessary, and is cooperative, positive, supportive, and offers enhancements. Adults provide young children with a range of experiences through open-ended, imaginative and heuristic (investigative) play.
- A nurturing environment reflects individuality, diversity and equality. It offers an opportunity for the child to learn about themselves, and others.

THE EMOTIONAL ENVIRONMENT

The physical and emotional environments are inextricably linked in nurturing care. It is the relationship that constitutes the emotionally nurturing environment. This includes strong partnerships between parents and professionals, behaviours, language/communication, how others are treated and how inclusive the environment is. It could be interpreted as the mood and atmosphere of the setting.

> Babies and young children are very perceptive and aware of the feelings and atmosphere around them. Relationships between adults and children, between adults and other adults and between children themselves all have an important role to play in developing the young child's sense of self and their understanding of how to interact with others.

> (Birth to three: supporting our youngest children. Learning and Teaching Scotland, 2005)

How to develop a nurturing emotional environment:

- Think about the relationships with the children, your colleagues, and the families.
- What behaviour is being displayed and mirrored upon – think about positive behaviour and positive language being used.
- Communicate effectively; foster a real culture of open communication.
- Inclusivity needs to be at the heart of all development of an emotional environment.

REFLECTIVE PRACTICE EXERCISE

Now let's consider the position of the child. Let's try to interpret some of the questions that the child may ask, or think about.

- Do you know my family and my circumstances?
- Who will I meet here?
- How will I be welcomed. What is the atmosphere like?
- How does everyone behave here?
- How will you help me become more confident and independent?

NURTURING CARE DOMAINS

As we mentioned at the beginning of this chapter, there are five domains of nurturing care (Figure 1.1):

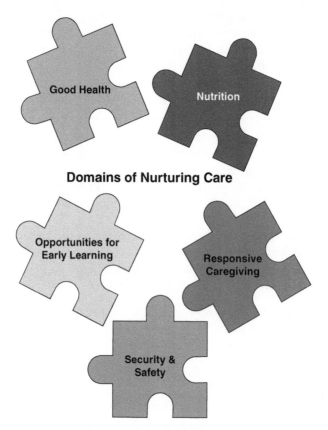

Figure 1.1 Domains of nurturing care (WHO, 2020)

The Domains of Nurturing Care by the World Health Organization (2020) explores that there needs to be an embedded aspect into childhood development and a maturational process in an ordered progress of perceptions, motor, cognitive, language and self-regulation skill. The acquisition from the life cycle builds on the foundations of the above nurturing care which is established during the time of early childhood. There is a multiple-faceted approach which influences aspects of early childhood, including the acquisition of competencies and skills, including health, nutrition, security and safety, early learning and responsive care giving including emotional support. Each of the domains is necessary for a nurturing care approach. Nurturing care reduces the detrimental effects of disadvantage on brain structure and function, and in turn improves the child's health, growth and development.

In terms of Early Childhood practice, the five Domains of Nurturing Care can be a useful tool to support reflective practice. Think back over the discussions in this chapter, what thoughts, questions, ideas have occurred along the way. The following Reflective Practice Exercise can be used as a reflection tool, a planning tool or even as an action plan to develop nurturing care approaches. Whether knowingly or not, the ethos of nurturing care is used and promoted by practitioners, professionals and services across the Early Childhood sector. The intentions to assist parents and other caregivers to provide attentive, loving and responsive care to their children are ones we can all agree with. Nurturing care ensures that all children can grow, thrive and flourish, are healthy, protected from danger and ultimately become confident learners who care about others in society.

REFLECTIVE PRACTICE EXERCISE: DOMAINS OF NURTURING CARE

As a professional within early childhood, let's position ourselves as advocates on how we advocate for nurturing in your setting.

- How are you relating your practice to the Domains of Nurturing?
- Have you managed to reflect on why nurturing is important? Are you able to discuss nurturing with your other colleagues?
- How do you make your setting nurtured and positioned around the child, family and professionals?

Think about your role currently how do you make sure that the child is supported with the five domains? Think about how you advocate for this within practice.

Using the grid below, consider the 'Domains of Nurturing Care', how would these relate to your own role, or the role of colleagues (Table 1.1)?

Table 1.1 Exploring the domains of nurturing care within the context of the professional services available to the children and family

Domain	Examples	EY practitioner	Family support	Health support	Leader/ Manager
Health	Family planning				
	Prevention – smoking cessation, alcohol/Substance use/Support				
	Antenatal/Postnatal care				
	Childbirth care				
	Immunisations				
	Disabilities care				
	Support for mental health				
	Early detection of illnesses				

(Continued)

Table 1.1   Exploring the domains of nurturing care within the context of the professional services available to the children and family (Continued)

Domain	Examples	EY practitioner	Family support	Health support	Leader/ Manager
	Integrated health care				
Nutrition	Maternal nutrition				
	Breastfeeding support				
	Family health and diets				
	Growth and development support				
Safety and security	Prevention of abuse/Neglect				
	Playful and safe environments				
	Prevention of family violence Sanitation/housing				
Responsive care	Skin to skin contact with the child				
	Affectionate/Secure adult caregiving				
	Relationships with others				
	Daily feeding routines				
	Involvement with others				
	Social support				
Early learning	Responding to the child's communication				
	Language stimulation through singing and talking				
	Exploration of the environment				
	Child's play				
	Quality day care				

CONCLUSION

In conclusion, Bavolek's research on nurturing care is not just about the physical care of the child, but that of the environment too. You could argue that this relates to the holistic approaches of the child and the environments that they are in. The importance of an enabling environment for nurturing is facilitated within it, but also by the many policies and laws that support and assist you as a caregiver in providing nurturing care (or indeed, do not, as the case may be).

It is important to discuss the environmental factors of nurturing and how this can enhance, or indeed detrimentally affect, the opportunities that children have. It is also, therefore, an important facet of the Early Childhood sector, to understand our roles, and how we support and enhance the Domains of Nurturing Care, with knowledge of areas such as:

• Children's and parent's rights
• Benefits and social welfare support

- Local provision of services for the child and the family (such as breastfeeding support)
- Appropriate and affordable childcare services
- What is available to the child regarding free entitlement for Early Years provision

However, enabling a nurturing environment goes much further than the policies and laws that assist the child's holistic development. It is also important that we each as individuals consider and reflect on the environments we provide, for the children and families unique to our communities. To go back to a quote we used earlier, it is vital that we begin with the premise that all parents want the best for their children:

> We need to begin with the firm belief that all parents are interested in the development and progress of their own children. Parents want to be effective advocates on their children's behalf.

> (Ball, 2004)

Looking for nurturing care is a natural impulse for children as part of human survival instincts. Likewise, it is natural for parents and caregivers to protect children. However, it is also recognised that this can be undermined by stressors and challenges. Poverty, domestic abuse, alcohol/substance misuse, mental health issues, fleeing from war and conflict and so on, can make it very difficult for some families to be able to care effectively for their children. Moving to a new house, changing jobs, new babies, marriage breakdowns, bereavements and illness etc., can all take their toll on family life. The aftermath of these situations makes nurturing care approaches even more of a necessity in the Early Childhood sector. Understanding the ethos behind nurturing approaches when supporting behaviours, considering transitions and creating supportive but flexible routines, for example, is a valuable toolkit in continuing to embed an empathic approach for children and families.

KEY QUESTIONS

In what ways can we use the understanding of nurturing theory to enhance our work with children?

How can our settings embed an ethos of nurturing for our children and families?

How can we practically demonstrate empathy within our practices and further in our communities?

FURTHER READING

Bradbury, A. (2022) Nurturing in the Early Years: What the science tells us. Early Education. Number 69. ISSN 0960-281X.

Conkbayir, M. (2017) *Early childhood and neuroscience: theory, research, and implications for practice.* London: Bloomsbury Publishing.

2

URIE BRONFENBRENNER (1917–2005)

By Tamsin Grimmer

CHAPTER OBJECTIVES

By the end of this chapter, you will be able to:

*   Know the key points of Bronfenbrenner's Ecological Systems Theory.
*   Understand that children do not grow up in isolation.
*   Acknowledge the importance of context within a child's life.
*   Recognise how adopting a loving pedagogy can support a child's ecosystem.

KEY DEFINITIONS

Listed below are the key definitions that this chapter will cover. Many of the words sound complicated, however, once they are defined and explained in context, Bronfenbrenner's theory will make sense.

Ecological Systems Model	Bronfenbrenner's original theory is often depicted by concentric rings around a child in the centre and it explains the many influences on that child.
Socio-cultural approach	An approach which takes into account the social and cultural environmental influences on a child. Bronfenbrenner's Ecological Systems Theory sits within this paradigm.
Bioecological Model	The Ecological Systems Model was renamed the Bioecological Model as he developed it over time.

Microsystem	The child's immediate context e.g. family or setting.
Mesosystem	Interactions between child's various microsystems.
Exosystem	The localised context within which micro- and mesosystems exist.
Macrosystem	Broader social, political and economic context and value and belief systems.
Chronosystem	Long-term context of historical changes and transitions.
Loving pedagogy	A child-centred approach underpinning all aspects of our provision which holds children in mind and enables them to feel loved.

INTRODUCTION

For many years, theorists and Early Years Professionals alike have debated long and hard over nature versus nurture. Is child development purely the result of children's genes and the biological differences they are born with, or do children develop in certain ways because of the environment and the experiences they have during pregnancy and early childhood? Without wanting to sit on the fence in this debate, I believe it is both, although genes begin the process of development, it is nurture and the environment around the child which has the biggest impact on our children.

Bronfenbrenner is a name that not all childcare practitioners will have come across; however, he was incredibly influential in changing the way that child development was studied, proposing that environmental factors play a major role in this. He attempted to explain both aspects of nature and nurture and how interconnected children's lives are through his theories (Bronfenbrenner and Ceci, 1994). He firmly believed that it is the context the child finds themselves in, which determines their development. Bronfenbrenner could be seen as the founder of keeping children at the centre of our practice as his theory demonstrates.

Children are affected by their socio-cultural context and the world around them in many ways. The Ecological Systems Theory can be used to help analyse the effects of these contexts on young children's lives. This chapter will explore Bronfenbrenner's theory and link it with other theories and research that complement it. It will also consider how we can relate his theory to our everyday practice and how his influence has shaped our understanding of how children develop and learn.

BIOGRAPHY

Urie Bronfenbrenner was born in Moscow, Russia, in 1917 and moved to the United States of America when he was six years old. He is famous for creating the Ecological Systems Theory, or as he later called it, the bioecological theory, which is a holistic approach to studying child development. He argued that people do not live in isolation but instead belong to a family and grow up having attended nursery or school and living as part of a community or neighbourhood. He called this the ecological system and labelled its parts the microsystem, mesosystem, exosystem, macrosystem and later, chronosystem.

Bronfenbrenner studied psychology and music at Cornell University and went on to complete a master's degree and PhD at Harvard University and the University of Michigan respectively. He began work as a psychologist, working for the military during World War II. After the war he mostly worked in higher education, as an assistant professor at the University of Michigan and a professor in human development, family studies and psychology at Cornell University, where he specialised in Child Development. His work was influential in the creation of the USA's National *Head Start Program* which aims to reduce inequality and support children living in poverty, and he is often attributed as one of the co-founders of this organisation.

Prior to Bronfenbrenner writing *The Ecology of Human Development* (1979), child development had mainly been studied in different subject areas, for example, within child psychology, sociology or anthropology; however, his theory demonstrated how all these different facets of the child were interconnected as part of one ecology and it was impossible to separate the child from the context they found themselves within. The Bioecological Model, as it came to be known, broke down barriers between these disciplines and enabled childhood to be viewed more holistically within the social sciences as one phase that ends in adulthood.

Bronfenbrenner spoke publicly about his concerns around society and was active in trying to improve many social issues such as the impact of inequality and urbanisation on children. He believed that, 'Children should be nurtured and educated to be able to maintain and strengthen their society' (Bronfenbrenner, 2005, p. 285) and saw family as the critical means in which to do this. He regularly engaged with policymakers and professionals with the aim of enabling his academic study to influence them (Hayes, O'Toole and Halpenny, 2017). His ideas were revolutionary at the time as he warned that society was in 'jeopardy' as a result of the major environmental changes taking place (Bronfenbrenner, 2005).

During his career he wrote hundreds of research papers and 14 books and received many honours and awards for his contributions to research. In his honour, the American Psychological Association created the *Urie Bronfenbrenner Award for Lifetime Contribution to Developmental Psychology in the Service of Science and Society* award which 'recognizes an individual who over a lifetime career has contributed to the science of developmental psychology and who has also worked to apply developmental psychology to society' (APA, 2021). In his personal life, Bronfenbrenner was married to Liese Bronfenbrenner and they had six children together. He died, at home, in New York in 2005, aged 88, due to complications relating to diabetes.

THE ECOLOGICAL SYSTEMS THEORY

Bronfenbrenner believed that the environment in which a child grows up will have an immense impact on their development and should be considered. He offers a theoretical perspective explaining how humans are affected by an interconnected system with many different parts or 'environments for human development' (Bronfenbrenner, 1979, p. 8). He keeps the child at the centre of his theory and discusses the processes and conditions that have an impact on them at different times. For example, there are many influences, such as their family, home environment or nursery setting which will have a direct or indirect impact on the child.

His theory has been drawn as a model with concentric rings, sometimes called circles of influence, with the child in the centre. Going outwards from the centre are different systems with differing amounts of influence on the child. They focus on children's lives in terms of the processes and conditions that influence them at different times (Bronfenbrenner, 1994). He gave each part a name and they have been described as layers in an onion (Buchan, 2013), nested systems or Russian dolls (Rosa and Tudge, 2013; Bronfenbrenner, 1999, 1979). The child is viewed as an active individual who can affect and alter their own environment (Papado-poulou, 2012) actively constructing it, rather than simply experiencing it (Plomin and Burge-man, 1991). The aim is to create a 'supportive ecology around a child' (Brendtro, 2006, p. 165) and viewing the child holistically, encompassing all influences on them (Figure 2.1).

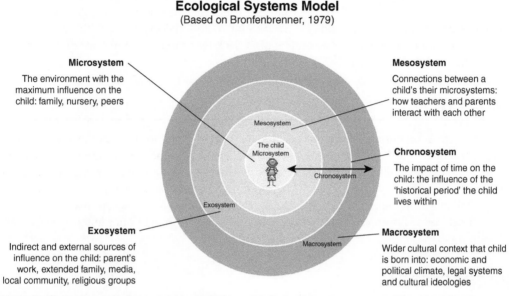

Ecological Systems Model
(Based on Bronfenbrenner, 1979)

Microsystem
The environment with the maximum influence on the child: family, nursery, peers

Mesosystem
Connections between a child's their microsystems: how teachers and parents interact with each other

Chronosystem
The impact of time on the child: the influence of the 'historical period' the child lives within

Exosystem
Indirect and external sources of influence on the child: parent's work, extended family, media, local community, religious groups

Macrosystem
Wider cultural context that child is born into: economic and political climate, legal systems and cultural ideologies

Figure 2.1   Ecological systems model
Source: Based on Bronfenbrenner (1979)

He later developed this theory into a more mature form, even renouncing parts of his earlier stance as throughout his life he revisited, revised and reflected upon previous versions (Tudge et al., 2016; Aubrey and Riley, 2015; Rosa and Tudge, 2013; Bronfenbrenner, 1999, 1995). The evolution of his theories being so extensive that it caused Aubrey and Riley to state, 'Bron-fenbrenner himself could be seen as one of his biggest critics' (2015, p. 120). In doing so, Bronfenbrenner models critical reflection and reminds us we are all constantly learning and evolving in our own understanding of the child. We will now examine each layer of his model in more detail.

MICROSYSTEM

The microsystem refers to the influences that 'affect an individual within their immediate setting' (Bronfenbrenner, 1979, p. 7) or in other words, those that are closest to the child and have a direct influence on them. For a young child this could include their family, home environment and early childhood setting or school. It is generally accepted that the microsystem has the greatest impact on a child, and they are actively constructing this environment rather than simply experiencing it. The aim is to create a 'supportive ecology around a child' (Brendtro, 2006, p. 165) which means adults should reflect upon a child's microsystem and ensure it is supporting the child. The influences within the microsystem are two-way, or bidirectional, meaning that children can also influence others.

MESOSYSTEM

The mesosystem relates to how each aspect of the microsystem is interconnected and cannot be separated (Bronfenbrenner, 1979). For example, how teachers and parents interact with each other has an impact on the child. As he developed this theory, he saw these systems as interrelated and impossible to isolate and he placed a huge emphasis on the role of the family in young children's lives (Seden, 2006).

EXOSYSTEM

The exosystem describes the indirect influences on a child from more external sources (Bronfenbrenner, 1977), for example, the mere fact that parents are working full time will indirectly affect the children, or an incident at the parent's work may mean they come home and are short tempered with their child. Therefore, as Rosa and Tudge indicate, there can still be a huge influence on the individual and they cite the example of a politician making decisions that will determine how a childcare setting runs and what they might offer in terms of care and education (2013).

MACROSYSTEM

The macrosystem is the cultural context that the child is born into, including the economic climate, legal, political and educational systems in place. These influence the family in many ways, for example, through culturally accepted or promoted parenting styles and also in terms of the underlying belief system or ideologies that the family adhere to (Rosa and Tudge, 2013; Bronfenbrenner, 1977). In addition, Servos et al. have found that a child's identity is hugely influenced by society and the cultural background that they are growing up within (2016) which confirms Bronfenbrenner's belief that the macrosystem plays a large role in shaping individuals as they develop. On the other hand, Evans and Price ask to what extent culture is responsible for identity formation as opposed to the role of self (2012). Thus the nature–nurture debate continues.

CHRONOSYSTEM

Bronfenbrenner later included the chronosystem into his model, which is considering the impact that time will have on the individual or in his words, 'the historical period through which the person lives' (1999, p. 20). He describes this as a 'crucial component' which must be considered (Bronfenbrenner, 1995). For example, as a child grows and develops, they will learn to respond in different ways to the environmental influences around them and significant events or transitions that occur throughout their childhood and life will have a profound impact on their development. For example, the coronavirus pandemic, known as COVID-19, will have significantly impacted children living through it. In addition, if Bronfenbrenner were writing today, I'm sure he would see technology, and social media, as having a profound impact on the child. Technology impacts all the systems and could be seen as positive or negative, for example, if a parent engaged more with their phone than with their child, this would have a negative impact, whereas, if a child were able to have more contract with extended family who perhaps live in a different country through video calling software, this could be a positive influence.

As part of his later work, Bronfenbrenner developed the process, person, context and time (PPCT) research tool in order for researchers to apply the bioecological theory in practice (1999) which he believed would validate their research and make the findings more accurate. His work has indeed been used by many authors; however, Tudge et al. suggest they are not always using it appropriately (2016). Despite this, Bronfenbrenner's work, both in terms of ecological and bioecological theory remains influential to date with many scholars using his theory as a framework for their research (Tudge et al., 2016; Rosa and Tudge, 2013; Pound, 2011; Darling, 2007).

REFLECTIVE PRACTICE EXERCISE

Having read about the ecological systems model, imagine the impact on a child in the following situations:

- Their parent has a new baby (microsystem).
- Their parent changes job which indirectly impacts on the child as their attendance pattern in their setting changes (exosystem).
- A new EYFS is published and their setting alters their policies and procedures (macrosystem).
- The child is growing up during a time in history experiencing a global health pandemic (chronosystem).

Bear in mind that all these things are interconnected and impossible to isolate from each other which exemplifies the mesosystem.

LOVING PEDAGOGY: PUTTING THEORY INTO PRACTICE

Bronfenbrenner's work resonates particularly for me and I have often drawn upon it when considering what constitutes a loving pedagogy. His theory firmly keeps the child at the centre and reminds me of the importance of always starting with the unique child. When we develop a loving pedagogy, we are keeping children at the heart of what we do, holding them in mind and promoting their best interests. This empowers them as they feel listened to, heard and are valued as part of our setting. It is as if in adopting a loving pedagogy we are putting Bronfenbrenner's theory into practice (Figure 2.2).

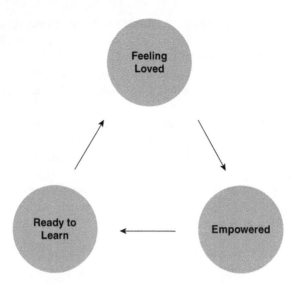

Figure 2.2   Empowering children through a loving pedagogy (Grimmer, 2021)

REFLECTIVE PRACTICE EXERCISE

We need to consider how we are nurturing the child and family and review our policies and procedures in the light of this. Here are some questions to reflect upon:

- Does each child feel listened to and valued as part of our setting?
- Do we respect individuality and our families' unique funds of knowledge?
- How do we demonstrate this?

Do our policies reflect our diverse families and explain our nurturing approach?

Within Bronfenbrenner's theory, our loving pedagogy can fall into place. The individual pieces that make up the context of the child, their family and wider society all add to the larger picture which helps us to see the child, with all their interconnected parts, more holistically. We can keep the child at the centre and value their contribution through our actions too, as we actively listen and offer advocacy and agency to the child and their family (Grimmer, 2021) (Figure 2.3).

Valuing the children, we work with:

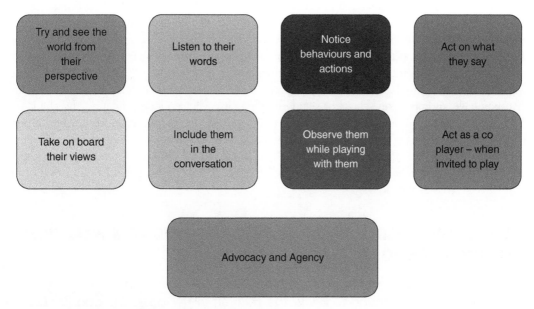

Figure 2.3 Valuing children we work with
Source: Developed by Grimmer (2021)

CASE STUDY: LOVING PEDAGOGY (FROM A PRESCHOOL)

Marlis: An Early Years Teacher

Our preschool has always kept children at the centre of everything we do. We believe that strong loving relationships between key people and children are vital and can enhance learning and development in early years. This loving pedagogy is written into our policies and evident in everything we do. A recent example of this is when we had a little boy who showed signs of separation anxiety from his mother, and extreme shyness and lack of confidence in social situations with peers. We realised that the people with the strongest attachments to him would be situated within his microsystem and so we worked together to support him to cope with his emotions, particularly when separating from his mother. We introduced the book, The Invisible String (Karst, 2018) which considers the connection between people who love each other, regardless of the physical distance between them. Each time he heard the story, the person reading with him would then encourage conversations about people close to him and feeling a connection even in times of separation. We also created photo key rings for our children to use as transitional objects and as a physical reminder of their connections with their loved ones. Excitingly, his keyperson witnessed him looking at his keyring with fondness in solitary moments and then seeking out other children directly afterwards.

When we relate the Ecological Systems Theory to practice, it highlights the importance of context and the impact that the immediate environment can have on a child. Each child brings to our provision their own unique funds of knowledge, background and culture. We can strive to find out about our children as individuals, as a member of a family and part of a community. We know that the microsystem of a child will have an impact on them, for example, close family members or early childhood setting. Whether they live in a city, town or the countryside will influence the child, as will their culture or any faith groups they belong to. In addition, when politicians make decisions that may have an impact on school or setting funding, this will also indirectly affect the child.

The role of the adult is to get to know the unique child and also to learn from them. When Bronfenbrenner refers to bidirectional or reciprocal interactions he describes them as, 'a process of mutual "education"; the child is "teaching" the adult, and the adult is "teaching" the child' (1990, p. 31). It's lovely to think of our learning from children and that they can enrich our settings and lives as we do so.

CASE STUDY: USING BRONFENBRENNER'S THEORY IN PRACTICE (FROM A SCHOOL)

Lauren is an Early Years Teacher in a school who uses Bronfenbrenner's theory as a way of really getting to know the children in her class. She doodles her thoughts about her children capturing a wealth of information (Figure 2.4).

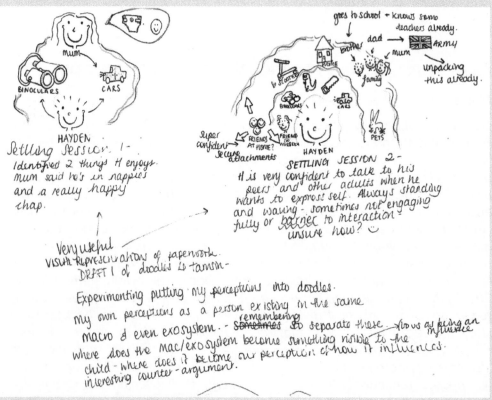

Figure 2.4   Bronfenbrenner theory in practice

(Continued)

As an Early Years Practitioner in whatever capacity I have worked, I use Bronfenbrenner's Ecological Systems Theory with each child as they come into our setting. I map out what I know of the children, be that mentally or physically through illustrations and notes, adding to it as they grow with us throughout their time at the setting. It is a fantastic example of how well we as practitioners know and understand the child and the context in which they exist, and an invaluable tool in supporting them throughout their learning journeys. This is a puzzle that as practitioners we naturally begin to piece together, however, viewing it through the lens of 'The Ecological System' allows us to collate our knowledge and have a concise, heuristic picture of the child (Figure 2.5).

Figure 2.5   The ecological systems picture of the child

Lauren has found using Bronfenbrenner's ecological theory as a focus for her observations a great way of considering the child holistically. It helps her to think about the influences on the child in their microsystem, mesosystem, exosystem and macrosystem. In this case, there are many direct influences on Hayden and Lauren has also included details which help her to engage him in class, for example, his pets, his interest in cars and tools as well as his links with the Army.

CRITIQUE OF HIS WORK

Bronfenbrenner has not been without critics over the years. Some arguments suggest that he only accounts for nurture in his model in the nature–nurture debate and nature plays a larger role than he acknowledges. Children are born with certain personalities or dispositions which will also have an impact on their development. Gray and Macblain (2015) have highlighted that Bronfenbrenner's theories can be criticised for not adequately acknowledging the psychological needs of children although as the ecological model places the child at the centre, it could be argued that it encompasses all needs that the child has, including psychological ones.

One difficulty with the Bronfenbrenner's theory is that it necessitates looking in great detail at all aspects of a child's life, which can be very difficult to do in practice. We do not know everything about a child, and we will not always be in a position to find out. In addition, it raises questions such as: 'What information is relevant?' 'Which information should I include or exclude?' and 'When should I stop gathering this information?' Acquiring this level of detail could feel unachievable.

Doherty and Hughes criticised Bronfenbrenner believing that more emphasis should be placed on the various interactions that occur throughout a person's life (2009), not just between the different systems. It could be argued that the chronosystem does this as it accounts for changes, events and transitions that occur over time or throughout a child's life. Therefore, when considered as a whole, the various systems that Bronfenbrenner details do indeed consider numerous interactions over time and perhaps his model is as broad as those who use it choose to make it.

In addition, it could be argued that many people do not use Bronfenbrenner's theory to its full extent, choosing only to focus on its child-centric notion rather than fully exploring all implications of his theory. Tudge et al. (2016) considered 20 publications whose authors claimed to base their research on Bronfenbrenner's theory and found only two had used it appropriately, leading them to state it was used as a, 'flawed heuristic tool' and that using it incorrectly 'prevents a fair test of the theory' (2016, p. 428). This echoes the research led by Tudge et al. (2009) previously, which also considered how scholars claiming to use Bronfenbrenner's theory had fared. They felt that it was vital that scholars should specify which version of Bronfenbrenner's theory they are using to avoid misleading their readers. Despite these criticisms, I believe his theory to be useful, even if used in their view superficially, as it can open our eyes to the important influence that context plays in a child's life and enable us to see a child as not growing up in isolation.

A FOCUS ON FAMILY

Bronfenbrenner's theory views the child holistically as part of a family and much wider community. It reminds me of the phrase that is often said to be an African proverb, 'It takes a village to raise a child', meaning parents and carers are not acting alone in bringing up children; they will have and need support from extended family and their community around them.

Over the past quarter of a century or so, family life has changed immensely. Adults are very mobile, often moving away from their childhood hometown to study or work. Many will move, not just within their local area, but nationally, and even, internationally as, with the increased global communications and infrastructure, the world feels a much smaller, yet better connected place. When Bronfenbrenner was first writing in the late 1970s, the world was a rapidly changing place and he recognised that families, which he viewed as vitally important, were breaking down and becoming more and more displaced or fragmented.

His theory is just as relevant today as recent research in the United Kingdom has found that 56% of parents with children under five experience loneliness when bringing up their children (Cottell, 2019). The research also found that parents on lower incomes were twice as likely to feel lonely than their more affluent counterparts. Where is the village for these parents and families? There are practical ways that we can 'be the village' and be part of the solution for these children and families in our own area, for example, through rallying around after a baby is born and organising a rota of meals for the new parents or doing the shopping for someone when you know they are looking after a sick child and will find it hard to get out. At work, we can look out for the parents and carers of our children and signpost to different organisations if they need help or offer a listening ear if they need to talk. We can also encourage a community feel in our settings, organising events where parents and carers can meet each other and generally assist parents in building a support network.

RELATIONAL PRACTICE

Bronfenbrenner believed that relationships were at the heart of child development. The parent and carer's roles were to nurture and care for their children and support them as part of their wider ecology. When a child is nurtured, this has a positive impact on them. Bronfenbrenner practiced what he preached and held people in high regard, once famously telling the vice president of the United States that he would have to call him back because he was in a meeting with a student!

In a presentation at a UNESCO conference, Bronfenbrenner outlines his position in a series of propositions. In the first proposition he talks about how children need to develop, 'intellectually, emotionally, socially and morally' in a reciprocal relationship over time with one or more people, 'with whom the child develops a strong, mutual, irrational emotional attachment, and who is committed to the child's well-being and development, preferably for life' (1990, p. 30). He is referring to a child needing to be part of a family who endlessly loves them unconditionally as the following quotation implies.

> What do I mean by '…an irrational emotional attachment?' There is a simple answer: '… Somebody's got to be crazy about that kid, and vice versa!' But what does 'crazy' mean? It means that the adult in question regards this particular child as somehow special – especially wonderful, especially precious, even though objectively the adult may well know that this is not the case. It is the illusion that comes with love – an illusion that flows in both directions. For the child, the adult is also special – someone to whom the child turns most readily in trouble and in joy, and whose comings and goings are central to the child's experience and well-being.

(1990, p. 32)

This is what I mean when I discuss adopting a loving pedagogy (Grimmer, 2021). Early Years professionals who love the children in their care, who will be there and act as a secure base for them. This reciprocal relationship needs to be at the heart of our practice and underpin everything we do in our settings.

REFLECTIVE PRACTICE EXERCISE

Consider a child you support. Use Bronfenbrenner's ideas to construct an ecology around the child. Start by drawing a series of five concentric rings (circles within circles). Label the inner circle with the child's name. Then working outwards, label each of the systems and consider who or what might influence the child at this level.

CONCLUSION

On researching this chapter, I came across a wonderful anecdote in Bronfenbrenner's obituary for the Association for Psychological Science, written by his friend and colleague, Stephen J. Ceci (2005). Ceci and Bronfenbrenner were meeting on a dull, rainy day in the 1980s and Bronfenbrenner turned up wearing what appeared to be a child's raincoat! He claimed it was his, however, Ceci insisted it wasn't and so he looked inside at the label (apparently, his wife used to name his clothing for him). They found it was, indeed, a child's raincoat that he was wearing – he had put on the coat of his secretary's eight-year-old son, who was off school that day and playing in her office! I really love the thought of this highly intelligent man, being scatty enough to not notice he was wearing the coat of an eight-year-old!

Bronfenbrenner touched the lives of the many people he met, and thousands of children he has never and will never meet. He remains influential with many scholars applying his theories or using them as a framework for their own research (Tudge et al., 2016; Rosa and Tudge, 2013; Pound, 2011; Darling, 2007). I have attempted to do this myself, by linking my ideas around developing a loving pedagogy (Grimmer, 2021) with his ecological framework. Bronfenbrenner's legacy lies in child centred practice, in recognising the importance of nurture and the influence that the social and emotional environment has on children's lives. His work will continue to make a difference in the lives of future generations and reminds us, despite the constant top-down pressure on our youngest children, that we must and should remain bottom-up and child centred.

The final words of this chapter are dedicated to Bronfenbrenner's epitaph (Brendtro, 2006, p. 165) which reads, *'Every child needs at least one adult who is irrationally crazy about him or her'* which I am sure you will agree, is a loving pedagogy in action.

KEY QUESTIONS

In what ways can we use the Ecological Systems Theory to enhance our work with children?
How can our settings become part of the solution for our children and families?
How can we practically demonstrate our loving pedagogy in our communities?

FURTHER READING AND RESOURCES

Hayes, N. and O'Toole, L. (2017) *Introducing Bronfenbrenner: A Guide for Practitioners and Students in Early Years Education (Introducing Early Years Thinkers)*. London: Routledge.

Sean McBlain's article for Parenta Magazine on Bronfenbrenner. Bronfenbreasnner: children's learning in a wider context. Available at: https://www.parenta.com/2018/09/01/bronfenbrenner-childrens-learning-in-a-wider-context/

Nursery World article by Professor Tricia David, Early Years Pioneers: Urie Bronfenbrenner. Available at: https://www.nurseryworld.co.uk/features/article/early-years-pioneers-urie-bronfenbrenner

3

PIERRE BOURDIEU (1930–2002)

By Kate Irvine

CHAPTER OBJECTIVES

By the end of this chapter, you will be able to:

- Develop an understanding of Bourdieu's theory of cultural capital including how it acts (often negatively) on learning and social mobility.
- Identify some aspects of cultural capital in action in ECEC that may be holding back the progress of children from less advantaged and more diverse backgrounds.
- Understand the importance of our values in practice and culturally relevant provision for children and families.
- Identify some practices in ECEC that have the potential to disrupt the negative action of cultural capital on young children and their families.
- Make links across some other established Early Years approaches and theories.

KEY DEFINITIONS

Cultural capital	The attitudes, dispositions and behaviours that wealthy classes have that enable them to progress well through education and in society and that perpetuate inequalities (Grenfell, 2006).
Scholastic fallacy	The systems by which schools and settings can often perpetuate social inequality while claiming to diminish it.
Field	An arena of society where social and cultural powers are enacted.

Doxa	The unquestioned or accepted 'truths', communication and codes of behaviours within a Field of society, e.g. early education, that are dominant.
Habitus	The socially and culturally ingrained behaviours and understanding of the individuals within a field (such as early education). These may or may not align or mirror those of the Field, its Doxa)
Symbolic violence	The negative action of the tension between the cultural capital of educational systems and settings and individuals that limits the achievement and development of children from socially or culturally diverse backgrounds.
Cultural arbitrary	The beliefs and social constructions that exist in the aspects of the curriculum or education system. Whose cultures are selected and reflected?

INTRODUCTION

This chapter unpicks the theory of cultural capital and its impact on children and families in the context of early education and care (ECEC), supporting practitioners with a deeper and practical understanding of the complex influences of our early education systems on children's learning and development. This chapter however also comes with a health warning in recognising that the interpretation of Bourdieu's theory of cultural capital through the standardisation of early childhood education is often a negative force for our children and families. It is only through taking time to understand what cultural capital is and how it interacts within the curriculum and practice that we can also come to understand how we might begin to resist and disrupt its negative impacts and the importance of provision that sustains children's cultural identities and experiences on learning and well-being.

CULTURAL CAPITAL AND PIERRE BOURDIEU (1930-2002)

Few of us working in ECEC in England had heard of French social philosopher, Pierre Bourdieu, until the country's school inspectorate, Ofsted, chose to add the notion of Cultural Capital as one of its criteria for judging the quality of provision in Early Years and schools in 2019. Although not wholly based in the Early Years, the theories of power and culture in society researched by Bourdieu have much to contribute to our understanding and practice in early education in ways that are more complex than they may first appear.

Underpinning Bourdieu's social theory is the recognition that children born into less affluent backgrounds attain less well compared to their better-off peers at all levels of education including the Early Years. In the English Early Years system this is seen in the statutory Early Years Foundation Stage Profile (EYFSP) assessment results at the end of the Reception year (age four or five) where the gap between the attainment outcomes of the poorest children and their peers is rising (Department for Education, 2019). Studies of communication and language levels at the age of two and on entry to school consistently show lower levels for children from lower income families, and that children who experience persistent disadvantage are significantly less likely to develop the language needed for learning (Communication Trust, 2017).

What we do in the Early Years really matters. Multiple studies, including the Department for Education's SEED reports (2015, 2017), Communication Trust (2017) and the influential Effective Provision of Preschool Education (EPPE) report, (Sylva et al., 2004) demonstrate the importance of high-quality early education particularly for children experiencing social disadvantage. Becoming better informed about social theory such as cultural capital in the context of our practices and provision supports practitioners to make sure that all children have equity of opportunity to learn and develop.

CULTURAL CAPITAL, WHAT IS IT ALL ABOUT?

THEORETICAL CONCEPTS

Cultural Capital is a term attributed to sociologist Pierre Bourdieu, to describe the unspoken or ingrained attitudes, dispositions and behaviours that the wealthy classes of a society have which enable them to progress well through education and the workplace; maintaining their social position to the detriment of the less wealthy and is the social mechanism through which division and inequality is perpetuated (Grenfell, 2006). Bourdieu based much of his research and theory on his childhood in rural France and his later experiences in Algeria, and it is also important to recognise the contribution of his colleague, Jean-Claude Passeron. Although mostly researched and published through the 1970s and 1980s, Bourdieu and Passerson's theories on social inequity have dominated social and political thought and anthropology ever since (Webb, Schirato and Danaher, 2002; Robbins, 2000; Grenfell, 2009). Their theories explain why social divisions are not easily eradicated by education alone, and crucially, for us as Early Years educators and carers, how we might prevent or even reverse its negative action on the children and families we work with.

SO, WHAT DOES BOURDIEU SAY?

The crux of Bourdieu's work around schools and education is his idea of 'scholastic fallacy' (Bourdieu, 1997a, 1997b, p. 50) and that schools and settings are not actually democratic places of meritocracy that they often claim to be (Grenfell, 2009). We can see this in the persistent gaps in education outcomes in all sectors including Early Years. According to Bourdieu the populist idea of formal education and raising educational outcomes as a way out of disadvantage is simply not true. It is a fallacy not only because it is manifestly more challenging for disadvantaged children to engage in education and achieve the curriculum outcomes compared to their peers but also that Bourdieu's theories show how standardised education systems also act cumulatively to reinforce this effect.

Bourdieu's educational research unpicked the social hierarchies of children within schools and the relative position of them to each other on the basis of their family income, types of family behaviours or parents with a university education (Webb, Schirato and Danaher, 2002). He showed how school policies and systems create an advantage for the already advantaged families to succeed, observing that while 'those with the necessary cultural dispositions from their family backgrounds found themselves as if to be a fish in water swimming with the current; those without such requisites had the opposite experience' (Grenfell, 2009, p. 440) (Figure 3.1).

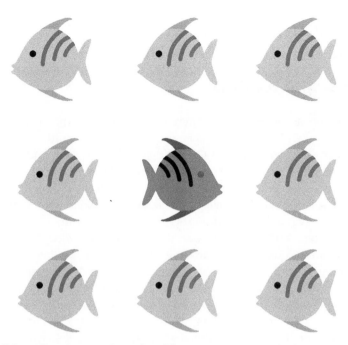

Figure 3.1   A fish swimming against the tide

So, rather than improving children's opportunity in society as schools are intended, Bourdieu's theory of cultural capital demonstrates an uncomfortable truth that our systems of education sustain the hierarchy of social divisions in society in our schools and settings (Robbins, 2000 'in' Fowler, 2000).

Practitioners will already recognise that some children arrive in our settings with the 'sort of' attitudes and dispositions, strong communication and some knowledge that enable them to get off to a flying start. Whether it is knowing how to 'play shops' or 'trains' or being familiar with simple routines and songs, these are the children most likely to leave our care having progressed the most. This is sometimes referred to as the 'Matthew Effect', the action of accumulated advantage that is seen in economics where the rich get richer, as well as in education. The term was first coined by another sociologist Merton (1968) and comes from the Bible passage in the book of Matthew: 'For to everyone who has will more be given, and he will have abundance; but from him who has not, even what he has will be taken away' (Matthew 25:29, RSV).

REFLECTIVE PRACTICE EXERCISE

- What were your own experiences of early education and starting school?
- Did you feel a sense of belonging or something less inclusive of you and your family experience?
- Which children in your setting might be thought of as 'a fish out of water'? and what are we doing to counter this?

HOW DOES BOURDIEU'S CULTURAL CAPITAL WORK TO ADVANTAGE THE ALREADY ADVANTAGED?

FIELDS, DOXA AND HABITUS

Human societies operate across many different environments known as 'fields' in cultural capital theory. These can be physical environments such as nurseries, schools, hospitals or workplaces or notional sectors such as academic areas, e.g. science and health. A field is an arena in which economic, educational and cultural capital operates and is exchanged. In their iconic work *Reproduction*, Bourdieu and Passeron (1970) detailed how the field of education duplicates the existing social inequalities by operating under and reinforcing the same expectations and behavioural codes of the dominant parties of the existing social hierarchy. These (often unspoken) codes of behaviour, attitudes and knowledge are called the 'doxa'. Dress codes, uniforms, routines for managing children such as lining up, behaviour and disposition expectations, the subtlety of communication and language and humour, and familiarity of the environments and resources are all examples of the doxa of a setting in action.

All settings including Early Years settings have their own doxa, and these will replicate the cultural expectations of the prevailing class culture to a greater or lesser extent. Think about the expectations for welcoming children, sitting still at circle time, lining up for lunch or to go outside to play, or perhaps even the way we soothe or calm an upset child and the domination of particular cultures in the stories and songs that are common in the Early Years. Bourdieu and Passeron (1970) show that although outwardly education systems claim to raise the learning outcomes of children, this is not equitably accessible by all children. Those who already have the 'right' understanding, experiences and dispositions become even more advantaged in the system. Bourdieu and Passeron (1970) called the codes of behaviour that children already have and bring to our settings their 'habitus'. Children who arrive in school with a habitus that matches the doxa (within the field of the school) are much more likely to feel attuned and motivated, attain praise and achievements and progress much more easily than the children with a different habitus.

Supporting children's cultural capital might seem like a pretty good idea for educationalists and is promoted by the English inspection system, Ofsted, as something positive, but it is not that simple. Bourdieu discovered we cannot simply teach or increase cultural capital. The accumulation of cultural capital starts from birth and is dependent on the nurture, time and personal investment of the family and social experience and cannot be attained by proxy by learning the 'right' knowledge or behaviours. Bourdieu and Passeron (1977) explain how many educational systems give enhanced status to the knowledge and dispositions from the dominant classes, calling this type of knowledge a 'cultural arbitrary' and explain how it is through following and mirroring the 'cultural arbitrary' that schools and settings become complicit in an illusion of creating equality and limiting the progress of some children. Bourdieu and Passeron (1977) labelled this effect 'Symbolic Violence' due to the way it can damage the educational success of some children.

One example of Bourdieu's cultural arbitrary, and, it could be argued, symbolic violence, in action is in the fallacy of the idea of the 'word gap' and the way we are encouraged by policy makers to employ early language interventions that take children out of the quality interactions in the mainstream provision their peers continue to benefit from. These types of interventions often focus on specific vocabulary and are predicated on the infamous, and now discredited,

Hart and Risley (1995) study. The Hart and Risley (1995) study looked at the numbers of words heard by young children from different socio-economic groups, claiming that wealthier families exposed their children to many millions more words by the age of 5 and that this is critical to achievement in school. Of course, we know that language development is vital, but the Hart and Risley (1995) study has subsequently been shown to be unreliable by a number of scholars including Baugh (2017) and Johnson (2015) who not only demonstrate its inaccuracy but also highlight its inherent racial bias that perpetuates the myth of a cultural deficit in young Black children from low socio-economic families in particular. While Early Years educators need to be aware of children's developing language and communication, some vocabulary interventions encourage the pathologisation of children with different backgrounds (Dudley-Marling, 2020) and disproportionately impact negatively on the learning experiences of children from low income and immigrant families (Cheruvu, 2020).

REFLECTIVE PRACTICE EXERCISE

- What might be some of the unspoken expectations or routines of your daily routine?
- Do all the children you work with understand and follow these easily?
- What unique cultures, knowledge and skills do your children and families bring into your setting?
- How do we value the unique experiences and language systems of children?

WHAT DOES EARLY YEARS PEDAGOGY OFFER US TO COUNTER THE IMPACT OF CULTURAL CAPITAL?

At first glance, Bourdieu and cultural capital theory seems to offer a somewhat fatalistic and depressing view about our efforts as educators. Although Bourdieu failed to offer solutions to the negative action of cultural capital in education systems, helpfully there are other social and pedagogical theorists who do.

Like Bourdieu, Brazilian social philosopher Paulo Freire, researching on a different continent, also outlined how schools are not the places of social liberation they are often claimed to be and crucially provides a way forward. Writing in 'Pedagogy of the Oppressed', Freire coined the term 'banking concept of education' (Freire, 1970, p. 49) to demonstrate how the oppression of marginalised groups is maintained by educational systems that focus on the teaching (and memorisation) of the formal knowledge of the dominant sections of society, but unlike Bourdieu, he researched how critical action to counter this can be developed through pedagogies that include the authentic participation of all communities and the 'cultural synthesis' of the lived experiences of the children.

The role of pedagogy in defining and controlling knowledge, education and power has also been explored extensively by modern philosopher, Henry Giroux. Like Freire (1970), Giroux (2011) sees opportunity in what he calls 'critical pedagogy' to act against the inequity (and the fallacy) of education and meritocracy. Giroux (2011) calls for 'educators to connect classroom knowledge to the experiences, histories and resources students bring to the classroom', and become active and critical agents of society (Giroux, 2011, p. 8). These are concepts that are already familiar to most Early Years educators and at the heart of much of our practice. Giroux is critical of the way that the reduction of education success to measuring facts and knowledge has infiltrated all sectors of education, from the curriculum in settings and schools to training of educators. As Early Years practitioners and leaders, understanding the work of Giroux, like that of Freire and Bourdieu, helps us become mindful of how we might interpret and use assessment frameworks and interventions, and most importantly, to take informed steps to disrupt the negative impacts, enabling children to feel valued and successful.

THEORY INTO PRACTICE

HOW DO WE BECOME CRITICAL PEDAGOGUES?

Just because Bourdieu and others show that cultural capital cannot and should not be taught doesn't mean we should not introduce them to Mozart or Michaleangelo. Such works are incredibly enriching; however, Mozart and Michelangelo alone, without a provision that celebrates children's own cultures and accommodates the habitus they bring into our settings, will always be limiting. Freire (1970) suggests that the answer to the inherent inequity of educational systems is for educators to engage in dialogue with communities and empower them to be active in their own thinking and critically aware. This philosophy resonates with Early Years approaches such as Te Whariki from New Zealand and the *Hundred Languages of Children*, from Reggio Emila, Italy. This can also be explored further in Chapter 7.

Rather than selecting the knowledge to impose on children and communities, the pedagogies of Reggio Emilia and Te Whariki reject a knowledge-focused curriculum and embrace uncertainty. Both trust children as capable agents of learning through their interconnectedness with their communities and worlds in contrast to notions of adding cultural capital through teaching specific knowledge and behaviours. Such systems offer alternative ways of viewing children and schools as successful.

Cultural capital in the Reggio model is not knowledge imparted to a child but can be seen as a motivation, an experience already within the child to be enhanced. In Reggio settings, pedagogical choices of teachers are linked directly to their sociological understanding and the inclusion of children's cultures and experiences (Goouch, 2010). This is both democratic (Moss, 2019) and emancipatory by giving pupils control over their learning. The Te Whariki Early Years curriculum of New Zealand, the name of which means 'woven mat' when translated from its Maori, also supports educational possibilities through the empowerment of a child's family and community in the setting and a focus on relationships and holistic development. Te Whariki includes familiar socio-cultural and developmental learning theories but is deeply rooted in a holistic vision of childhood that respects individual and communities' cultural heritages (Marek, 2019). Respect for a child's choices and strengths is also found in the pedagogy of the High/Scope Foundation in which children are encouraged to make and carry out their own learning plans and are given time and support to reflect on what happened with a concept of the capable child at its core. Understanding the features of approaches such as these are good starting points for early educators interested in countering the negative impact of the action of cultural capital in our early education systems and curriculums.

Solutions can also be found much nearer to home for practitioners in the English EYFS, with a focus on the overarching principles of the unique child, positive relationships and enabling environments, and an interpretation of the statutory framework through a lens that respects and actively includes and values the child's community and family. High-quality learning environments and practices that put the child in control of their choices and explorations support a child's well-being, independent motivations and explorations (Whitebread, 2014; Hodgeman, 2012) and support the statutory characteristics of effective learning, attributes identified in the Tickell report (2011) as vital to acquisition of other forms of knowledge. These characteristics are the dispositions and attitudes that support children to be interested, involved and agents of their own development (Stewart, 2011) and fuel children to show interest, sustain attention, bounce back from setbacks, and to have and adapt ideas (Moylett, 2014). They are mirrored implicitly and explicitly in many early education systems around the world including Te Whariki and Reggio Emilia as well as Montessori and High/Scope approaches.

CRITICAL PEDAGOGY AND CULTURALLY SUSTAINING PEDAGOGY

For many children however, child-centred pedagogy may still not be enough to resist and disrupt the impact of cultural capital in education on young children's learning experiences. The context of ECEC is changing and not always for the best. A growing global political push for formalisation of learning content and pedagogy in Early Years creates a climate that is both dismissive of individual personal and cultural experiences (Brown, 2020) and dismissive of ECEC pedagogy and play (Bold Beginnings, DfE, 2019). This can be seen acutely in England where the inspection system misinterprets cultural capital and ever more academic outcomes are required of young children in its high stakes accountability system. Not only do such policies ignore the capabilities and knowledge within the child but the pursuit of such standardised learning outcomes which prioritise one form of learning over others encourages practitioners to find deficits in children to be measured and fixed. Government-funded initiatives often dictate that children are removed from the group for interventions and denied the quality Early Years experiences that research shows to have an impact (Brown, 2020). Thankfully, ECEC practitioners can overcome this through critical reflection and the development of pedagogies that nurture and sustain children's cultures (Cheruvu, 2020).

In addition to ECEC practices that build on strengths and engage with communities and celebrate their uniqueness, histories and express their capabilities there are also practices that actively challenge the status quo. Antiracism is a concept that explicitly challenges the systemic, passive and racism of all aspects of society. It recognises a duty not only to challenge racism in all its forms but to also introduce children to other lives and experiences, 'being anti-racist is a dynamic process, something we do every day, moment to moment, in our interactions with children and the experiences we offer them. One-off gestures and good intentions are not enough; this needs to infuse every aspect of our practice' (Henry-Allain and Lloyd-Rose, 2021). ECEC practitioners can challenge the negative impact of cultural capital by responding to the inequity evident in the experiences of children and families of colour, those with disabilities and the LGBTQ+ community. Representation and authentic inclusion of all families in our settings matters.

Longitudinal studies such as the EPPE (Sylva et al., 2004), A Mandate for Playful Learning in Preschool (Hirsh-Pasek et al., 2008), The High Achieving White Working Class Boys study

(Pascal and Bertram, 2016) and the UK government's own Studies of Early Education and Development (SEED, 2020) demonstrate significant benefits to children's later academic, well-being and social outcomes through Early Years pedagogies and high-quality child-centred provision.

LINKING TO PRACTICE

My own Masters' research explored practices of Early Years practitioners that mirrored the practices identified as impacting on children's learning and countering the deficit model of children and families. Giving a voice to and explicitly valuing and celebrating all children's lived experiences balance the doxa of the school, instead of creating one that creates advantage for one.

In Early Years we can counter the impact of cultural capital in the education system right from the start. Baby room practitioners that take time to learn the words and tunes of the family to sooth a child, create environments that reflect the colours and textures and offer familiar smells and tastes of the home immediately create the circumstances for children to flourish. An environment that is alien will be harder to a child to settle into and this applies for five- and six-year-olds as much as young babies. Authentic engagement with families matters and so does making it integral to provision and practice every day, not just a 'diversity day' or an 'African art week'. Home visits are important for getting things right for all children of all ages in Early Years. These visits are our very first opportunity to say to a child and family 'I value you' and to learn about their strengths and lives to build on in our provision and ideally are not just one-offs when a child starts a setting. The COVID pandemic of 2020 and beyond may have made visits in person impossible, but it also opened new ways of using technology for communicating with and valuing families and ongoing authentic dialogue.

REFLECTIVE PRACTICE MATTERS — WALKING THE WALK OR TALKING THE TALK?

Stopping to consider why a child may not be accessing the curriculum or experiences we offer is vital to reflective practice. Phrases like 'tuning into children' and 'playing alongside' are much used in Early Years but how often are they really enacted? Reflective practice means asking questions of ourselves, our judgement, our biases and professional knowledge, not just children.

The misappropriation of so-called 'important knowledge' as cultural capital, which has unfortunately gained traction in recent English educational policy, as a solution to social inequality does not correspond well to theories of culturally sustaining pedagogies that are shown to impact Black and minority ethnic pupils in schools (Demie, 2018; Lane, 2007) or the supportive parental relationships and child-led pedagogies that impact most on children living in poverty (Dudley-Marling, 2020; Pascal and Betram, 2016; Sylva et al., 2004).

Rather than highlighting 'what works', the theories of Bourdieu show us not only what 'doesn't work' but what can even be damaging to children's development and learning. Understanding Bourdieu means that we view cultural capital as something to be aware of; take steps to minimise the impact of our settings for children living in poverty and from backgrounds different to the dominant social classes; and we avoid conflating it with the enriching experiences we offer our children and families.

> **KEY QUESTIONS**
>
> Is there anything we could change to include the habitus of all the children more equally?
> How are lived experiences of all our children and families explicitly valued in our settings?
> What steps might we take to be able to see all children as capable learners?
> What are our practices which create a more inclusive culture for all?

FURTHER READING AND RESOURCES

Alanen, L., Brooker, E. and Mayall, B. (2015) *Childhood With Bourdieu*. Basingstoke: Palgrave McMillan. Springer.

Kjørholt, A. (2013) Childhood as social investment, rights and the valuing of education. *Children and Society*, 27, 245–257.

Moss, P. (2019) *Alternative Narratives in Early Childhood*. Abingdon: Routledge.

Nuxmalo, F. (2020) *Disrupting and Countering Deficits in Early Childhood*. New York, NY, Abingdon: Routledge.

Urban, M. (2017) We need meaningful, systematic evaluation, not a preschool PISA. *Global Education Review*, 4(2), 18–24.

Webb, J., Schirato, T. and Danaher, G. (2002) Understanding Bourdieu. Allen and Unwin. Crows Nest Australia p. 22, 59, 107, 116.

United Nations Convention on the Rights of the Child (1989) Available at: https://www.unicef.org.uk/what-we-do/un-convention-child-rights/ [Accessed 29 December 2021].

4

FRIEDRICH FROEBEL (1782–1852)

By Meredith Rose

CHAPTER OBJECTIVES

By the end of the chapter, you will:

- Recognise some of the key aspects of Froebel's theory, including gift and occupations, unity and connectedness and relationships.
- Explore how Froebel's ideas impact upon practice in the Early Childhood discipline
- Discuss the centrality of play in Early Years practice today.
- See connections between Froebelian principles and other existing practices within Early Years.

KEY DEFINITIONS

Gifts	A set of resources including cubes, spheres and cylinders which can be used in a number of ways, to help children to 'explore aspects of maths, architecture, engineering and science' (Froebel Trust, 2021).
Occupations	Materials which help children represent aspects of their lives and encourage creativity. For example, mud being made into cakes, or paint being used to create a picture to tell story.
Play-based learning (pedagogy)	Play-based learning promotes holistic development by providing opportunities for children to actively engage with people, objects and the environment which helps them provide a sense of the world. The practitioner's role is to facilitate the learning environment and provide scaffolding to assist the children to develop mastery skills.

Play	Play is one of the most complicated things to define.
	Play provides opportunities for children to explore ideas, concepts and develop relationships while being immersed in experiences.
The role of play in learning	'Learning through play happens through joyful, actively engaging, meaningful, and socially interactive experiences' (Lego, 2017, p. 6).
Observations	The way in which we capture and make sense of what we have seen, and heard, when we work with children which helps us to plan and provide the learning opportunities for children. Observations can be formal, informal, written or remembered.
The child as a unique individual	Each child has their own identity, character, interests, skills and motivations.
Interconnectivity	The way that one experience has connections to other aspects of their lives and learning.
Provocations	A provocation is something that provokes interest, thoughts or connections. For example, a camera with film in it might provoke children to explore and ask questions about its use and differences to cameras that they are used to. The term which originates from the Reggio approach, but a provocation is useful for expanding learning and providing open-ended experiences with little intervention from adults.

INTRODUCTION

PLAY-BASED LEARNING: FROEBELIAN PRINCIPLES

The principles, examples, case studies and reflective activities are present in this chapter to help you see how the Froebelian approach is relevant to practice today. You may get to the end of the chapter and realise that there are aspects of these that you can use in your own setting, alongside other established practices that already work for your children. Consider that theories and approaches can be used as a 'pick-n-mix counter', once you have a good understanding of them, as it is commonplace to see practitioners and settings using a blend of approaches as their practice evolves.

Froebel's ideas have long been recognised as important for children's play, and he argued that 'play is the highest expression of human development for it alone is the free expression of what is in the child's soul'. He created the concept of kindergarten, meaning 'the children's garden'.

In this chapter, we will explore the principles and relevance to practice for children, practitioners and parents; practitioners are anyone who has a role in planning or leading play. Froebel's ideas were focused upon the child taking the lead in their play and learning by exploring and experimenting, while adults provide a scaffolded learning environment. Froebel's principles were centred around the ideas of having an interactive educational environment, which was completely different to many philosophers of that time, who believed children should follow a very strict adult-led learning regime.

Play is a human right and is evidenced in the UNCRC conventions (UNICEF, 1989) and the Salamanca statement (1994). Highlighting the centrality and power of play is one of the responsibilities of the Early Years sector, especially as there are increasing pressures to measure learning. Providing an environment that responds to a child's uniqueness is essential to ensure that your practice is inclusive and continues to be responsive to the developing child.

Froebelian practices, despite being over 100 years old, continue to work in harmony with children and their natural desire to explore, experiment and make connections to aspects of their lives. That is not to say that practitioners only need to understand and use one pedagogical approach, but finding the approach that works for your children, your own beliefs and those of your setting can be a complex process which takes time, reflection and dedication. As practitioners there are many influences from the different nations with the United Kingdom and our international counterparts, it is sometimes hard to know which approach to choose.

WHAT DO THE FROEBELIAN PRINCIPLES LOOK LIKE IN PRACTICE?

Over the last two years, there has been a renewed focus and energy upon unity and connectedness to our environments and to one another. As a society, we think about sustainability and or our role within the environment. Children are naturally inquisitive and should be supported to understand that our actions have consequences for the world we live in.

By using Froebelian principles in your practice, you can provide children with an array of opportunities and experiences that are developmentally informed.

In days gone by, pets in nurseries were a regular occurrence. Children gained experiences of considering and caring for another living being, and this benefited children in a range of ways, including empathy, trust, being kind and thinking about the diet and exercise requirements to keep the pet healthy. Some nurseries still have a connection with living things but there are many ways to achieve this.

- Houseplants inside the nursery
- Opportunities to grow and cook their own food or visit places that grow food, such as the local allotments and farms.
- Helping children observe nature and their surroundings throughout the seasons.

As a practitioner, you can also use opportunities in the wider community to create relationships with people and make new connections. Intergenerational projects have shown that there are emotional and physical health benefits for all participants as evidenced in the Channel 4 series *Old People's Home for 4 Year Olds* (2019).

Consider the following reflective practice exercise.

REFLECTIVE PRACTICE EXERCISE

As a practitioner, which of the following feels most in line with your practice:

- Creating opportunities for children to explore and process their understanding.
- Creating a 'product' such as a picture or a model for the benefit of the adults.

BIOGRAPHY

Froebel is recognised internationally as the founder of kindergartens.

Froebel's pedagogy focused upon four main areas:

- Child-centred learning – Putting the child as the first consideration for planning environments and learning opportunities.
- Manipulation of materials – Block play has been a core for Early Years settings and allows children opportunities for sorting, naming, positioning and repositioning shapes to create or recreate 'ideas' from their own lives. You will often see children use a range of shapes to create houses, cars or things that are familiar in their everyday lives. These experiences help children to consider shape, size and special awareness.
- Sensory development – Being able to explore, experiment and use all the senses in multiple environments is a key consideration for practitioners.
- Creativity within the child – Opportunities to explore and create in many different ways.

Froebel also created:

- Gifts – these were to help children understand size, shape and dimensions. These gifts encourage open-ended play.
- Occupations – malleable materials such as paint, dough and... were provided so that children could express themselves. Process of enjoyment rather than production.

Table 4.1 indicates some of Froebel's ideas and how these are still relevant in today's practices and provide children with opportunities to problem-solve and be creative.

Table 4.1 Using Froebel's theories

Froebel's ideas	Practice today	Sustainable alternatives
Gifts were originally wooden blocks of different shapes and sizes	Provide children with blocks that range from very small to large scale. This will provide a range of challenges and promote problem-solving and a range of body movements requiring agility and coordination. Provide children with a space to store the blocks.	Box play ensure that children have a good supply of cardboard boxes of different shapes and sizes. Discuss where the boxes have come from and where they can be recycled.
Open-ended play	Provide loose materials to support children to make choices and decisions which will support children's symbolic thinking.	Provide opportunities for children to collect their own sustainable resources. These could be recycled or repurposed materials.

REFLECTIVE PRACTICE EXERCISE

Consider the following:

- Can you walk around your setting and identify the gifts and occupations available?
- As a practitioner, are you confident with indoor and outdoor environments with the children? For example, do you see opportunities or challenges when it rains?
- Do the methods that you use to observe the children help you capture children's learning? What other methods of observing and assessing are available to you?
- Does your setting offer opportunities to use a range of gifts? What could you introduce to develop what you already offer?
- Are these gifts used to provoke children's interest? How?
- Are these accessible to the children? If not, how could this be achieved?
- Are these resources offered as a support to target-specific skills? Or, are they used to offer opportunities for the children to experiment and explore with?
- Consider what opportunities the children have for dealing with risk and challenge. How do you feel when the children want to take risks?

The choices you make about your practice and how that evolves is dependent upon many factors, including:

- Your own pedagogical beliefs and those who you work alongside
- The children and families that you work with
- The approaches used to observe and assess children's development

There have been many other children-centred educational philosophers over the 180 years such as Montessori, Reggio Emilia and the Waldorf Steiner method. There are a range of Early Years settings across the United Kingdom that focus upon one set of principles, and these may be adapted to their current practices or values.

If we look at the Froebelian principles, you may see connections to other theorists' ideas.

- Montessori – The environment should support the needs and interest of the child, whereas the adult should provide support in a manner which is sensitive and allows time for a child to engage to their own satisfaction (Montessori Society, 2021). Froebelian practice advocates opportunities for children to make decisions, choices and be child-initiated.
- Steiner – A focus on open-ended resources is crucial for exploration and to support the development of the child's imagination. Froebelian practice also advocates those opportunities to connections to the environment (both indoor and outdoor) we live in is essential.

- Reggio Emilia approach (developed by Loris Malaguzzi) – Children can build their own learning and the role of the adult is to support them in their efforts. A facilitation approach is appropriate rather than teaching. In Froebelian practice, this might be visible when children use loose parts to create or represent their ideas in symbolic play.

However, Froebel's ideas have particular significance to practice today due to the focus upon the unique child by the EYFS (DfE, 2021) and the increased awareness of emotional health and well-being. Supporting children's intrinsic desire to learn and individual interests has become a key consideration when choosing pedagogical approaches.

FROEBELIAN PRINCIPLES

Table 4.2 identifies the principles for practice but also examples in practice and considerations for practitioner working in the sector. The principles have significance to all of us working with children and families.

Table 4.2   Froebelian principles for practice

Principles of practice	Examples in play	Relationship to current practice	Relevance to practitioners	Relevance to parents
Childhood is seen as valid in itself, as part of life and not simply as preparation for adulthood	Play should be fun, engaging and allow children to become immersed.	Provide a broad range of experiences and opportunities.	Talk about valuing play and young childhood with others. Protect and celebrate play opportunities. Use research and policy reports as part of staff development events.	Celebrate play with parents. Explain the significance of children being immersed in play and the holistic benefits. Discuss the criticality of the Early Years and provide copies of reports and research which highlight the value of play.
The whole child is considered to be important	Provide experiences that connect to the children's own lives and provide multiple opportunities for learning, rather than be specific about the intended outcomes.	Observations of the child are key to provide experiences and opportunities that provide appropriate challenge to support each area of development. Partnership working is a key	Provide an environment that responds to children's interests and it will have benefits for their holistic development. Reflect on the language you use and the way in which you talk	Talk to parents about play experiences and key concepts. Explain how the activities have multiple benefits for the child and how these concepts are interconnected. 'Charlie was using the water tray

(Continued)

Table 4.2 Froebelian principles for practice (Continued)

Principles of practice	Examples in play	Relationship to current practice	Relevance to practitioners	Relevance to parents
		principle of the EYFS. Each child is unique and should be considered for their uniqueness.	about children and their uniqueness. Reflect on the play environment and how it supports the children's interests and motivations.	today and was really engaged when trying to sink or float objects. Charlie also made a series of "boats" from different materials and problem solved effectively'. Engage with parents to show an interest in their cultural practices and home life.
Learning is not compartmentalised, for everything links	Encourage children to experiment, explore and test, bring equipment together, for example, sand and water, water and dough. Learn from the children. What are they drawn to? What opportunities do they have? Is the space effective? What could make it better?	Enquiry-based learning. Opportunities should be provided both indoors and outdoors to provide children with a broad range of experiences. Development Matters (2021) Birth to Five Matters (2021)	Ensure that children have access to familiar objects and continual provision. Provide opportunities to ensure that children can revisit activities and complete them to their own satisfaction. Are you familiar with EYFS-Development Matters/Birth – 5 matters – Guidance?	Remember that parents see their own child's development, but they may not understand the terminology or processes of 'evidencing' development as you do. Plan your approach to talking to parents carefully. Provide opportunities to answer questions about aspects of practice but remember not all parents will want to do this.
Intrinsic motivation, resulting in child-initiated, self-directed activity, is valued.	A consideration for continual provision is helpful alongside the practice.	Ensuring the enabling environment responds to the children's needs and interests. Provide appropriate support based on the needs of	Observe carefully and ensure that you note what the children are drawn to and how they are engaged with an experience. Share your observations with the other	Continually engage with parents about what their children's interests are.

Table 4.2 Froebelian principles for practice (Continued)

Principles of practice	Examples in play	Relationship to current practice	Relevance to practitioners	Relevance to parents
		the individual child.	practitioners. What are their perceptions?	
Self-discipline is emphasised (Self-regulation is also discussed as part of self-discipline)	Provide opportunities where children can make decisions, choose how to use resources. Provide children with the tools to manage their environment independently.	Provide opportunities to self-regulate and make decisions. Discuss how you feel and provide children with the language to express their feelings and help them to articulate their emotions. Be a role model.	Engage in discussions with other practitioners about self-care, self-discipline. Celebrate 'failures' and 'achievements' visibly. Help children see how you deal with a range of emotions and situations.	Discuss what their child development. 'Today, Charlie used Please and thank you at snack time', 'Charlie knew when he was getting tired and spent some time in the chill out area.'
There are specially receptive periods of learning at different stages of development.	Play starts at birth. Providing a language-rich environment from the very beginning will have benefits for the rest of the child's life and all areas of learning. Play opportunities should be appropriately challenging but scaffolded with the child's unique abilities in mind.	Provide children with opportunities to return to activities and objects to help them master skills. Children need opportunities to test, explore and experiment and opportunities to build on previous experiences is essential.	Practitioners will rely upon their deep knowledge of child development to make the best decisions to ensure that the provision for the child is sufficiently challenging but is still accessible.	Engage in conversations about development and be clear about the difference between the sequence and rate of development.
What children can do (rather than what they cannot do) is the starting point in the child's education.	Praise children for effort at each stage of their learning. Use positive language when talking about children's achievements, and you will notice that children will do the same.	Provide children with opportunities to see when you experience successes and failures.	Ensure that you the language you use about children is positive. 'Charlie you have worked so hard today and persevered', rather than 'Charlie, you've spent ages doing that and you still haven't finish it'.	Provide clear factual information to parents about their child's development using positive language. Avoid being drawn into comparisons with other children including

(Continued)

Table 4.2 Froebelian principles for practice   (Continued)

Principles of practice	Examples in play	Relationship to current practice	Relevance to practitioners	Relevance to parents
	Role modelling.		Modelling behaviour and language that praises effort rather than achievement is useful. Are there opportunities for parents to ask questions and clarify their understanding?	siblings or friends. Are there opportunities for parents to ask questions on your website?
There is an inner life in the child, which emerges especially under favourable condition	Show interest, take your time. Listen for cues from the child and take the lead from their conversations. If the child shows an interest in shells in the sand, … If the child shows you a picture, take interest and ask them to tell you about the choices that they've made in producing it.	Using your knowledge of the child, you can prepare an effective enabling environment. Think carefully about the way that you present materials and encourage children to engage in the spaces.	**Observing** children and their engagement in play opportunities. Seeing the unique child will provide you with the best opportunity to support them.	Share your observations with parents and encourage them to do the same.
The people (both adults and children) with whom the child interacts are of central importance	Provide frequent opportunities to support the child about their lives, experiences and relationships, using a range of experiences. Example stories which involve different families. Talk about love, friendship Block play – children will	Good practice….	Use activity bags as a method to help parents with your interest at your setting. Today I have been using the blocks to make a model of my house. Today, I have been baking and here is the recipe…. Reflect on your relationships with children and their	Invite parents to stay and play to help you build effective relationships. They will then see the approaches and strategies being used. Provide opportunities to share information about the child's interests and experiences.

Table 4.2 Froebelian principles for practice (Continued)

Principles of practice	Examples in play	Relationship to current practice	Relevance to practitioners	Relevance to parents
	represent their lives in block forms which form a great start for discussion.		families. What makes you feel uncomfortable? How can you overcome these difficulties? Professional Love by Dr Jools page.	
Quality education is about three things: the child, the context in which learning takes place, and the knowledge and understanding which the child develops and learns	Provide opportunities that will help children revisit an experience repeatedly and master skills. Cooking, sharing food and eating together are good opportunities to experiment, create and share experiences.	Enabling environment both indoors and outdoors	Use the spaces available both in the setting and the community. Use the community spaces, places and people as an extension to your setting. On the way to the park what signs do we see, what do they mean?	Share your approach to planning, observation and assessment. Provide the information in a clear to show why you have provided the opportunities and how you support the children learning by providing a rich environment.

Source: Adapted from Bruce, 1987, 1st edition and 2015, 5th edition…Early-education.org

As a practitioner, you are likely to work with other colleagues who have had different practice experiences to your own. With that in mind, the reflective tasks are here to help you consider your approach in supporting a new member of the team.

REFLECTIVE PRACTICE EXERCISE

1. A new member of staff will be joining your team in two weeks' time. They have worked there for five years and have developed their skills and expertise using a range of pedagogical approaches.

   How can you effectively **prepare** them for joining the existing team, who have developed their practices around Froebelian principles?

   a. How could you ensure that the new practitioner settles and **adapts** to your practices?
   b. How could your team learn from their experiences?

   (Continued)

(Continued)

    c. What are the benefits of understanding a range of pedagogical approaches?

2. You approach the manager of the nursery and suggest a different method for observing and recording children's development. The manager and several practitioners refer to 'targets' and 'progress'. You don't like this approach as you feel it hurries the children through childhood.

    a. What evidence could you use to help them understand your point of view?

    b. Why does the language being used matter?

    c. What should replace 'targets' and 'progress'?

Now, can you apply the principles of Froebelian practice to this case study?

CASE STUDY

Background. *Charlie's family have recently moved to the area and are unfamiliar with what it has to offer to Charlie who's four and Mia who's two years old. Charlie lives with his parents and grandparents who have been eager to get to know the nursery practitioners and other parents.*

As Charlie's key worker, you are developing an understanding of Charlie's motivations and interests. Charlie engages in conversations with the other children easily and has quickly made friends with two other children, who attend nursery on the same days. Recently the children have begun role-playing and share an interest in dogs. All three children have pets at home and have much to say about their four-legged friends. The children can be seen taking the dogs to the vets and comforting each other, when one of the dogs is ill. They have been observed taking the dogs for walks, making obstacles courses for exercise, making prescriptions, giving medications and answering the surgery phone.

REFLECTIVE QUESTIONS

1. *Which materials and experiences could you use as provocations around the nursery to support these children's interests?*

    a. *As a practitioner do you feel confident in your practice indoors or outdoors?*

    b. *How might this impact upon the children's experiences?*

When you have observed Charlie, you notice that the majority of the time is spent outdoors and engaged in pretend play. Charlie also likes cooking in the

(Continued)

mud kitchen and making meals with his friends. He organises the chairs and asks his friends to 'come and get your dinner'. While 'eating' Charlie pours water for his friends and one child gets up to leave the table. Charlie quickly asks, 'where're you going…you didn't ask if you can go!'. He begins to cry, and one child tells him 'he's gone to play'. Charlie protests 'but he hasn't eaten his dinner'. Charlie is upset as the children don't seem to understand his family's 'normal' rules from home. The children and adults would all sit and eat together, talking about their day. All other activities including watching the TV stopped.

REFLECTIVE QUESTIONS

1. *As a practitioner, how could you help children understand and show respect for different family practices?*

   a) *Which Froebelian practices would this connect to?*

RELATIONSHIP TO CURRENT PRACTICES

WHY DOES A HISTORICAL THEORY MATTER NOW?

As Early Years Practitioners we are in a very privileged position to work with children and their families. The children that you work with are the citizens of tomorrow, and your contribution is crucial to their journey through their early years. The children and the families that we work alongside are also privileged to have practitioners who engage in continual professional development. The passion and enthusiasm in Early Years settings never cease to amaze me.

Early Years is an ever-changing landscape which requires a great deal of expertise, energy and enthusiasm. As Early Years practices evolve, the environment in which we work is influenced by political and societal changes, some of which are easier to adapt to. In recent years the United Kingdom has seen a significant increase in the interest and adoption of forest schools and similar outdoor learning environments. The evidence suggests that children engage with the outdoors, and it offers unique opportunities for children to be creative and express themselves. These concepts are not new and have been adopted from our European counterparts in Denmark.

Forest schools and outdoor learning environment help children experience and connect with nature, while also providing opportunities to become independent and take care of themselves. Children will have first-hand experiences of the changes of the seasons and how to keep warm on a cold day, or use shade to stay cool. Children may be able to cook outdoors and use tools and fire and as a consequence how to manage risk for themselves. When practitioner provides opportunities and environments where children can explore, experiment and experience real life, these activities will inevitably support holistic development (Table 4.3).

Table 4.3 The relationship between the Forest school principles and the Froebelian principles

Forest school principles (Forest school association)	Froebelian principles as above (Bruce)
Principle 1: Forest school is a long-term process of frequent and regular sessions in a woodland or natural environment, rather than a one-off visit. Planning, adaptation, observations and reviewing are integral elements of Forest school	The whole child is important
Principle 2: Forest school takes place in a woodland or natural wooded environment to support the development of a relationship between the learner and the natural world	Self-discipline is emphasised
Principle 3: Forest school aims to promote the holistic development of all those involved, fostering resilient, confident, independent and creative learners	Learning is not compartmentalised, for everything links

Quality education is about three things: the child, the context in which learning takes place, and the knowledge and understanding which the child develops and learns |
Principle 4: Forest school offers learners the opportunity to take supported risks appropriate to the environment and to themselves	What children can do (rather than what they cannot do) is the starting point in the child's education
Principle 5: Forest school is run by qualified Forest School practitioners who continuously maintain and develop their professional practice	The people (both adults and children) with whom the child interacts are of central importance
Principle 6: Forest school uses a range of learner-centred processes to create a community for development and learning	The whole child is important

TENSIONS AND DILEMMAS TODAY

Despite the changes that Early Years has faced, the bedrock of Early Years of practice is **play**, and this should be protected and celebrated at every opportunity. Play is undervalued and largely dismissed as unimportant. However, developing a deep and expert understanding of children and their development is informed by experiences, training and reflective practices. The **value** of these professional skills cannot be underestimated.

Sahlberg and Doyle (2020) argue that Children's lives are changing and the time to play is decreasing. Ramsey (2014) highlights the significant impact that our lives are having on children and recognises that play deficit disorder is a concern not only in England but in many areas of the developed world. Children need opportunities to play and 'lose their sense of time. Play can be chaotic, messy and loud and is full of surprises' (Baker and Abernethy, 2003).

REFLECTIVE PRACTICE EXERCISE

Consideration to help practice evolve in your setting:

As a result of these reflections, what changes could be made to make the environment more child-centred and encourage multiple learning opportunities?
Do you need to discuss these with other practitioners in your setting?
Do you need to discuss or persuade your setting to try a different approach to an aspect of practice?

CONCLUSION

At a time when the world is recovering from a global pandemic, many of us need to heal and have found ways to deal with our experiences. Play in all its forms and definitions is critical in this process for children and adults alike. Many of the things that adults enjoy and engage in are play but due to its status, we may not recognise it as such.

Play is important as my life as an adult not only because it's part of my profession but because of its power. Play is the thing I return to when I need space to think and when I need space to figure out complex issues; play is where I go to relax and enjoy spending time with others. Play is critical in my life! Unfortunately, many adults avoid play and see it as something less valuable than other forms of engagement. It could be argued that adults are missing out on a range of extremely valuable opportunities in their lives, if they do not play!

As society looks at ways to protect and care for our environment and becomes more sustainable, the Froebelian practices are also applicable in our lives as adults. We are the custodians of our world until we hand it onto the next generation. Being role models and supporting children to be creative in their thinking and approach to challenges may well hold the answers for many of the difficulties we face today, including climate change.

Next time you hear someone dismiss play as just 'child's play', be ready with a response! Talk about play, shout about play, celebrate play in all its glory!!

KEY QUESTIONS

In what ways can we use Froebel's theory to enhance our work with children?
How can our settings embed certain principles of the Froebelian approach for our children and families?
How can we practically demonstrate our Froebelian pedagogy in our Early Childhood communities?

FURTHER READING

Tovey, H. (2016) *Bringing the Froebel Approach to Your Early Years Practice*. London: Routledge.

Bruce, T. (2012) *Early Childhood Practice: Froebel Today*. London: SAGE Publications.

Bruce, T., Louis, S. and McCall, G. (2014) *Observing Young Children*. London: SAGE Publications.

5

JULIE FISHER

By Ruth Swailes

CHAPTER OBJECTIVES

By the end of this chapter, you will be able to:

*   Recognise the links to Early Childhood practice through the theoretical perspectives of Julie Fisher.
*   Consider the role of the practitioner starting from the perspective of the child in Early Childhood practice.
*   Understand the influence of transitions in education from Early Years to Key Stage One.
*   Understand how a holistic approach to early childhood education supports young children and their families.
*   Reflect upon the importance of play in Key Stage One.

KEY DEFINITIONS

Play

This is complex to define as different authors and researchers have provided a variety of definitions. Fisher identifies a range of characteristics which are universally agreed:
*   Play is an activity done for its own sake.
*   The process is more important than the product or goal.
*   Play engenders a sense of agency and control.
*   Play offers opportunities for creativity and flexibility.
*   Play gives children many opportunities to test out theories of the world and how it works.
*   Play is enjoyable.

Child-led learning	Hands over the control to the child, opening a multitude of learning opportunities; it is often spontaneous, unpredictable and challenging to observe and assess. Children-led learning develops children's independence and has no specific set of predefined outcomes.
Adult-led learning	Focuses on a narrow set of objectives and helps children to concentrate on an adult-set agenda, it introduces children to learning that they may not otherwise discover by themselves.
Adult-initiated learning	The objectives for the learning belong to the adult, but there are opportunities for children to own some of the process and outcomes. These should be meaningful, open-ended challenges which allow for a degree of flexibility in approach and outcome.
'Schoolification'	As the importance of early childhood has been recognised by successive governments in England, so has the increase in policy directing practice. It is argued that this directive style of policy has caused early childhood practice to become more formalised with an emphasis on adult-led practice. This style of practice is not supported by contemporary research and that of Bruce.
Neoliberalism	Over the past 40 years and successive governments, the United Kingdom has followed a political ideology called neoliberalism. In early childhood this has positioned parents as consumers and children as future investments; encourages market competition (the growth of private day care); standardised curriculum and it is argued a 'top down' pressure to address standards.
Child-centred	An approach which puts the child's developmental needs at the heart of practice.
Self-regulation	Involves children's developing ability to regulate their emotions, thoughts and behaviour to enable them to act in positive ways towards a goal.
Executive function	The skills which provide the capacity to plan and meet goals, display self-control, follow multiple-step directions even when interrupted and stay focused despite distractions, displaying cognitive flexibility.
Metacognition	An awareness and understanding of your own thought processes.

INTRODUCTION

You may already be aware of Julie Fisher's work, including her pioneering research on effective interactions and the process of transition from Early Years to Key Stage One. Fisher advocates for a truly child-centred approach in early childhood with the practitioner seeing their role through the child's eyes. Today, Julie Fisher is an independent Early Years advisor and visiting Professor at Oxford Brookes University in the United Kingdom. Her interests and experience span working with children within education from three-year-olds to children aged 12. More recently Julie's work allows us to consider the role we play in children's effective learning through our interactions with young children as well as carefully planning their transitions from Early Years to Key Stage One.

Nurture and well-being are important factors in children's ability to learn effectively. A child who is comfortable and secure is more open to new experiences. Ferre Laevers likens the child who is secure and demonstrating high levels of well-being to 'a fish in water' (Laevers, 2000).

The child is secure and comfortable. Young children require emotional support to be able to maintain a healthy balance to learning. Research tells us that when developmentally appropriate practice is applied (Copple and Bredekamp), meaningful learning takes place and when there is joy (Pritchard, 2018), unsurprisingly, children will engage more readily and learn from their environment more effectively.

Play still has an important role for children in Key Stage One; however, a neoliberal approach to early childhood education has introduced a wide spectrum of measurement, performativity and marketisation (Lundahl, Erixon and Holm, 2013) which has led to practitioners and leaders in school becoming increasingly anxious about making time for play and child-initiated learning. Learning through play is not straightforward and many people regard play as frivolous and less effective than direct instruction. Fisher argues for an effective balance of play and adult-led instruction. Play is a vehicle which allows children to develop language skills, communication and opportunities to make sense of the world when implemented effectively. Such playful approaches allow practitioners to build upon children's unique skills, knowledge and understanding.

The chapter provides a short synopsis of the following key elements of Fisher's work:

- Exploring play in Key Stage One, the importance for the child and some of the potential issues for the teacher
- Child-centred approaches to transitions for the five-year-old child into Key Stage One
- Effective interactions and their impact on children's learning
- Strategies to consider when developing a balanced approach to Early Years and Key Stage One pedagogy, based on Julie Fisher's work.

BIOGRAPHY

Professor (Dr) Julie Fisher is a well-recognised researcher and author within the field of early childhood education. Julie has taught children from 3 to 12 years of age and has been a headteacher of two urban, multicultural schools. She lectured in Early Childhood at the University of Reading then went on to become a Local Authority adviser for 11 years in Oxfordshire. More recently Julie is an independent Early Years Adviser and is a visiting Professor of Early Childhood Education at Oxford Brookes University. Julie has been the national chair of several Early Years organisations including the National Association of Early Years Inspectors, Advisers and Consultants and the national Early Childhood Forum. Throughout her work, Julie draws on her own research which continues to keep her grounded with practitioners and children. Julie's work explores child-centred pedagogy, the tension between developmentally appropriate practice and external pressures in English education, transitions and effective interactions between practitioners and children.

THE IMPORTANCE OF PLAY IN KEY STAGE ONE

One of the central themes to Julie Fisher's work is that our pedagogy should be rooted in our understanding of child development, rather than the current political orthodoxy. In her most recently published work the second edition of *Moving on to Key Stage One*, Julie reflects on the increasing pressures teachers in the Early Years sector now face and how the political landscape has changed since the first edition of the book was published in 2010. Back then in the United Kingdom there was a growing desire to build upon the effective practice in Early Years Foundation Stage (EYFS) and to try to bridge the gulf between the pedagogy and practice at end of the Foundation Stage and the beginning of statutory education in Key Stage One which had been identified by teachers, successive governments and National Foundation Education Research (NFER) in their research on transition (NFER, 2005). However, a change in the government and political direction in 2010 led to much of the work which had begun on making transition as seamless as possible being lost. A new agenda of 'school readiness' began in earnest. This theme was further developed by the Inspectorate in England, Ofsted, who published 'Are you ready?' in 2014 reflecting on the changes in pedagogy at the end of Reception, and the narrative became increasingly focused on preparation for the next stage of education. Julie is passionate about putting the child at the centre of all pedagogical decisions from the title of her first book *Starting from the child* it is obvious that this is fundamental to her approach to learning. She argues that children do not change into different people in the weeks it takes to transition from the end of the Foundation Stage to the beginning of Key Stage One, and the needs of five- and six-year-olds are very similar, yet all too often our expectations of children change at this point.

WHY PLAY?

Julie argues passionately and unashamedly for play in the Key Stage One classroom but does not shy away from tackling the very real fear that this strikes in leaders, heads, and some teachers. Fisher believes that children in Key Stage One deserve to have opportunities to access high quality play as the means through which they find stimulation, well-being, and happiness, and through which they grow physically, intellectually, and emotionally (Thomas and Harding, 2011). Play is an integral part of a child's exploration and learning, and as well as enjoyment and motivation, it offers children opportunities to learn and develop vital life skills. Play teaches children to deal with uncertainty and develop creative ways to be able to deal with these further (Mardell, Lynneth Solis and Bray, 2019).

Fisher also recognises that not only do some leaders fear play or think of it as being frivolous and no longer necessary for children in Key Stage one, but that some parents and teachers also hold the view that school should not be about play, but 'hard work'. As a result, in many schools play is left at the door when children leave Reception and enter the highly structured world of the National Curriculum. Misconceptions about play and misunderstandings from education colleagues and parents fuel the idea that play is a waste of learning time. Yet this viewpoint is very misguided. Fisher recognises that children in Key Stage One benefit from further opportunities for learning through play, and this helps to support a smooth transition from the Foundation Stage.

Our current approach to earlier formalisation in England is quite unusual in terms of international education, where the benefits of play are widely recognised in many other countries, and formal education often begins at the age of 6–7 years.

THE ROLE OF PLAY IN SUPPORTING SELF-REGULATION AND EXECUTIVE FUNCTION

There is a growing body of research and acknowledgement both within the United Kingdom and internationally that high-quality play has significant benefits for learning, and that the impact of this is significantly improved when the adults involved are highly skilled, experienced and well trained and understand their vision for children (Callanan et al., 2017). The recognition of the importance of engagement and enjoyment in developing children's motivation in turn, encouraging greater concentration and perseverance (White et al., 2017), and deep-level involvement (Laevers, 2000) is widely accepted.

The UK government has begun to recognise the importance of self-regulation, executive function and metacognition in developing children's learning, and play is an effective vehicle for these important skills. Whitebread (2012) highlighted the critical role of play in supporting children's language development, self-regulation and executive function. They argued that 'central to development are the executive functions of the brain, which encompass cognitive flexibility, inhibition and working memory, as well as more complex functions such as capacities to problem solve, reason and plan. The development of language is central to the whole process, through the channels of pretend play and the imagination, very young children can think and reason about experiences and ideas in sophisticated ways'. There is a growing body of research highlighting the importance of developing self-regulation and executive function and the long-term impact of developing skills such as perseverance (McLelland et al., 2012) and metacognition (Ornstein, Haden and San Souci, 2010) by the age of six.

WHAT DOES EFFECTIVE PLAY LOOK LIKE?

More recent work commissioned by the Lego Foundation in 2021 explores the five characteristics of playful learning experiences, which help children grow and thrive. The evidence suggests that children learn best:

- When their minds are actively engaged.
- They can meaningfully connect the play to their lives.
- They are socially interactive.
- They can test things out.
- There are no spoilers beforehand, making play surprising.

Let's have a look at these five characteristics in greater detail:
Five characteristics of playful learning experiences to support child growth and to be able to thrive:

1. **Being joyful** – Being joyful is about the joy of discovery. Joyful play sparks the brain's rewards centres, triggering a feel-good chemical called dopamine. Higher dopamine is linked to better memory, attention, creativity, mental flexibility and motivation.
2. **Meaningful** – Making sure that playful learning is meaningful, like seeing a horse in a field and being able to see a horse in a picture book. Being able to draw those connections expands children's knowledge of the world. It opens many different areas of the brain: motivation, sense-making, reflection and memory.
3. **Actively engaging** – The child is really involved in an activity by taking charge of their learning. Child's application by being able to make decisions and pushing away distractions 'executive control' – this is how we focus, plan, remember instructions and juggle tasks.

4. **Iterative practice and creativity** – When children keep adapting and improving their skills, ideas and activities, they are starting to fire up reward and memory networks. In the longer term, that is linked to flexible, innovative thinking.
5. **Socially Interactive** – Being able to play with others and have fun, more importantly it helps build healthy relationships. The social aspect is important for better mental health, as well as learning about empathy and preparing the brain to deal with everyday stresses and challenges through a child's life.

(Lego Foundation, 2021)

Considering the above information, play offers Key Stage One children the opportunity to develop attitudes, skills and understandings that can't easily be adopted through an adult-initiated planned activity. Fisher argues that play offers children an element of control and a degree of flexibility which is not possible through teacher-directed activities. Being able to set their own goals and objectives allows children to become more independent and take learning further than a narrow set of learning objectives defined by their teachers. The process of learning is not limited or constrained by pre-determined outcomes, and this allows children to be inventive, curious and daring. The role of the adult here is to facilitate, to support, encourage and develop through highly skilled interactions. In the second edition of *Moving on to Key Stage One* published during the pandemic in 2020, Fisher acknowledges that more than ever before we need to review our practice to meet the needs of children in a changing world affected by COVID-19 and that providing opportunities to learn through play in Key Stage One is one of the best ways to meet the needs of this unique group of children who need to make sense of the world and feel some agency and control at this time.

THE ROLE OF THE ADULT IN TEACHING AND PLAY

One of the misconceptions which persists about learning through play and child-initiated learning is that the child is in complete control and there is little or no adult input. Some people believe it means that the child has total freedom and that any interactions from the adult are 'interfering' and inherently bad. Fisher is very keen to dispel this myth and is clear that the most important and precious resource in the classroom are the adults. The best learning environment alone will not compensate for poor interactions and ineffective teaching. The Researching Effective Pedagogy in the Early Years (REPEY) study is clear that it is not enough to create a stimulating environment and let children play. Staff need to actively teach the children, which means modelling appropriate language and behaviour, sharing intelligent conversations, asking questions and using play to motivate and encourage them (Siraj-Blatchford and Sylva, 2002).

Fisher recognises that there are aspects of the formal Key Stage One curriculum that play alone does not teach (2020a), and the skill of the effective Key Stage One teacher is to identify these and to adapt their role accordingly. Skills such as handwriting, phonics, reading, writing, knowledge and understanding of historical, geographical, creative and scientific concepts and elements of mathematical development require adult-initiated learning, but can also be embedded and enhanced through playful learning opportunities. Play still has a role here in embedding and consolidating knowledge. Fisher examines the different roles the adult takes, depending on whether learning is adult- or child-initiated and argues that there are similarities in the range of skills required for both, but there are different purposes for the child-led agenda.

Child-led learning capitalises on children's natural ways of investigating the world, the adult makes informed decisions about when to interact and when to observe and their role is less predictable than in adult-initiated activities; this is because the learning is not always predictable, through child-led learning children have a safe space in which they can experiment, practice and rehearse what they already know and have been taught, and the adult has to be alert in order to be responsive to this and to be 'warmly attentive' (Fisher, 2016; Vermes, 2008). Experiences repeated in this way help to strengthen the connections between new learning and what is already established (Conkbayir, 2017).

Fisher carefully examines the different roles the adult takes depending on the nature of the learning taking place. By reflecting on the core purpose of each activity practitioners are encouraged to reflect on their role within the specific context.

During adult-led activities the adult has a specific outcome in mind and therefore has greater control; this is often more attractive to adults as it can give the impression of being more effective; however, Fisher reminds us that this can be challenging because so much depends on the children's individual responses to set challenges and activities and there can be a tension. For example, the adult can have a learning intention in mind, the child may try to take the learning in a new and different direction and the teacher must take a decision whether to allow that or to try to bring the activity back to the original learning intention.

If we consider the role of the adult as more fluid, moving from adult-initiated to child-led and back again as appropriate, this can lead to increased flexibility of learning, deeper understanding, greater levels of satisfaction and agency for the child and teacher alike. This requires skill and confidence, and the adult has to be unafraid to switch from facilitator, to instructor, to observer, to commentator and back again as the situation develops. Julie's work here on effective interactions in 'Interacting or Interfering' provides a wealth of practical guidance, support and suggestions on ensuring that adults are confident to know when and how to interact, ask questions, comment or be silent.

Of vital importance is respect for the child and their knowledge. Each child will bring their unique perspective to every learning situation. What Fisher asks us to do is to 'wait, watch and wonder' before jumping in. Our instinct as practitioners is to offer support, to guide, direct and take the learning in the direction we have in mind. By stepping back, watching what is happening and taking care to consider whether adult intervention would improve or enhance the learning we learn more about the child and can adapt our teaching as necessary. Gentle commenting, thinking aloud, verbalising our own learning and thoughts, and making connections to previous experiences and learning help children to understand our thinking, and to understand that adults also have to consider and ponder ideas as part of the learning process. This modelling is empowering for children, if adults don't know all the answers, it's okay that they don't either!

REFLECTIVE PRACTICE EXERCISE

Consider the following:

- Taking on board the characteristics of playful learning have you noticed how these play out within your own practice?
- Consider a typical day in your setting, what is your role in the children's learning? What's the balance between adult-initiated and child-initiated activities?

(Continued)

(Continued)

- Do you allow yourself time to wait, watch and wonder, and do children explore activities, ideas and concepts before you interact and pose questions?

THE POLITICAL CONTEXT

We know that play supports the foundations of children's well-being (Howard and McInnes, 2012). But politically there seems to be a movement to take play and child-initiated learning away from the Key Stage One classroom and to an extent more recently the pressure is pushing down even further into Reception, with the perception of an increasing expectation from Ofsted of a subject-based curriculum. It is important to remember that the children entering this key stage are only five years old and some of them will have just turned five. In many countries, these children would still be attending Kindergarten and experiencing a play-based curriculum for another 18 months.

Researchers have highlighted the strong correlation between some of the most vulnerable children in our schools and their level of risk when play is absent. The early school starting age in England is somewhat anomalous when we look at schools all over the world. Up until the start of the National Curriculum in 1988 this was not particularly problematic as teachers developed their own curriculum and Reception teachers were free to plan a curriculum they deemed appropriate for their children, and at this time most children entered school in the term they were five rather than in the September of the academic year when they were five. The introduction of the National Curriculum with its subject-based learning inevitably led to some Reception teachers being pressured to try to make this work for Reception children and this was highly problematic. The introduction of the Foundation Stage curriculum in 2000 was a mixed blessing. Increasingly schools were moving to a two-point or even single-point entry system leading to an increasing number of children starting school aged four, some only days after celebrating their 4th birthday. A more appropriate and balanced curriculum was welcomed, but with the accompanying Early Learning Goals led to inevitable pressure to ensure that as many children as possible achieved them regardless of their age and stage. Thus began the chequered relationship between early childhood pedagogy and assessment. On the one hand, a unique and distinct phase for our youngest children was a move in the right direction; on the other hand, the goals became another 'hoop to jump through'. Over the last 20 years there has been a continual power struggle between the needs of the child and the demands of external accountability agendas, and there is nowhere this has been more apparent than in Reception and Year One. The constant push from above to formalise, the 'schoolification' of early education has been a constant and ongoing pressure. Fisher doesn't shy away from tackling this tension head on. She continues to advocate for developmentally sensitive practice but recognises the bravery required to put child-centred pedagogy at the heart of learning because the current political agenda focuses on the curriculum rather than on research-informed pedagogy and the child.

There are schools willing to be bold and brave enough to stand up for this developmentally sensitive practice. Some schools use play at the start of Year One to support transition; others are brave enough to continue it throughout Year One and even into Year Two. This isn't without challenges. Curriculum and assessment pressures make allocating dedicated time for child-initiated learning difficult. Schools' ethos and culture are critical in enabling the effective implementation of play. This approach requires highly skilled teachers who are willing to be flexible and take risks. Teachers without any training or experience developing play in Key Stage One need the time and support to be able to learn. Leaders of schools will need to be comfortable and confident to articulate the impact of this approach and to give time and commitment to put it in place, and Fisher shares many examples from case studies to support colleagues in this area.

It is easy to see how the lack of high-quality opportunities for child-initiated learning in the Year One classroom compound the academic, social and emotional challenges in school for those children identified as our most vulnerable learners (Weisberg et al., 2013). It could be argued that children who are entering Year One currently need greater levels of support with transition, given the impact of COVID-19. Sriram (2020) explores critical periods of brain development and identifies a crucial period beginning around the age of two and concluding at around age seven. During this critical period, it's important to maximise children's potential by developing nurturing loving relationships, curiosity, emotional intelligence and a wide range of experiences, allowing children to focus deeply and become engaged and involved. High-quality play and interactions offer opportunities for all of these to be implemented.

The perceived shift politically towards a more formal, 'knowledge-rich' curriculum has led some schools to adopt an approach in Year One which is similar in style to upper Key Stage 2 and even Key Stages 3 and 4. Thus, making the move from a curriculum which is holistic with interconnected areas of learning developed through a balance of adult-initiated and child-led learning even more of a challenge. It is important to remember that the National Curriculum, which provides the statutory guidance for schools, sets out what must be covered in each key stage; it does not set out how it should be taught. At the time of writing there is an increasing feeling that Ofsted is imposing a particular approach on schools, but it is important to be aware of the wording in the Ofsted handbook (2021):

> Ofsted will not advocate a particular method of planning teaching or assessment; it is up to schools to determine their practices.

> Ofsted does not advocate that any approach should be used exclusively in teaching. Different approaches to teaching can be effective. What is appropriate will depend on the aims of a particular lesson or activity.

> We will judge schools taking radically different approaches to the curriculum fairly. We recognise the importance of schools' autonomy to choose their own curriculum approaches. If leaders can show that they have thought carefully that they have built a curriculum with appropriate coverage, content, structure, and sequencing, and that it has been implemented effectively, then inspectors will assess a school's curriculum favourably.

TRANSITIONS

Fisher's work on transitions draws on her experiences in the Oxfordshire transition project (2005–2008) and extensive experience of working with schools focusing on this area. A well-planned, effective transition should be as seamless as possible, so that rather than trying to bridge the chasm between EYFS and Key Stage One, we support children on a continuum of developmentally sensitive learning. By putting the child at the heart of our practice and looking at the process through the eyes of a child, it is possible to identify potential issues and consider how we might plan for and mitigate these. Fisher shares practical ideas about common issues and potential solutions. Transitions are milestone events for children and have a significant impact on their development; vulnerable children, who can find moving from the known to the unknown particularly challenging may need sensitive additional support at this time. Drawing on the work of O'Connor (2013), Julie highlights some of the potential vulnerabilities and uses case studies to reflect on how schools might overcome these. At the present time Reception and Year One are under the political spotlight more than ever before; the Ofsted focus on the links between the Early Years and Key Stage One curriculum, coupled with three statutory assessments in the first 24 months of school, means that there is a great deal of scrutiny, by empowering the professionals to place at the heart of transition practice to reflect on what a high quality looks like; Fisher reminds us that our greatest level of accountability is to the children and families we serve.

A high-quality transition recognises the importance of feeling 'known'. Birth to Five Matters Non-Statutory Guidance for the Early Years Foundation Stage (2021) states that the key to a high-quality experience for all children is to ensure continuity between the following:

- The home
- Key people
- Settings

The NFER research project into transition (2005) identified that transition is most effective when it is viewed as a process rather than an event, and Fisher identifies this as the first principle of effective transition. It's widely recognised that children will experience a number of transitions and changes in their lifetime and will need to learn to adapt and cope with change. Where this process takes place gradually and children are well prepared for the changes ahead, they are much more likely to be successful. It's vital to plan for a number of visits to new classrooms and to meet with new staff so that children begin to feel comfortable and confident. None of this can happen without support from the leadership team. This is Fisher's second principle of effective transition; it is a whole school process. All staff have to understand the importance of ensuring an effective transition and a gradual shift. Where leaders understand the importance of play and the need for resources time and training, the impact is likely to be more positive.

Transition should be positive and exciting, and it's important to think about this through the eyes of the child, and parents. Transition is unlikely to be successful if children and parents are not involved in the process, it's also essential to acknowledge that this is a transition for parents too. Involving all stakeholders in discussions, giving Foundation and Key Stage One staff chance to meet, discuss effective pedagogy and really plan for effective learning is far more likely to lead to a smoother transition for all.

Through the EYFS children are entitled to a curriculum that is based on their interests, developing from what they already know. Year One teachers should build on these starting points and nurture children's desires for learning, but this is only possible if teachers from both phases have the time to discuss what this should look like. It's important to remember the most valuable resource in any classroom is the teacher, and by investing in time for teachers to really discuss transition in depth, the process of moving to Key Stage One is likely to be more positive. Year One teachers and practitioners can then build upon children's starting points and continue to nurture each child's natural curiosity (Figure 5.1).

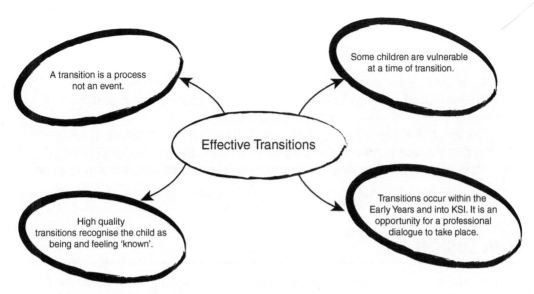

Figure 5.1   Effective transitions in early years and Year One

---

REFLECTIVE PRACTICE EXERCISE

1. How can we ensure that we are providing appropriate opportunities for a smooth transition?
2. How will you be able to support children who require an enhanced transition?
3. How will you ensure that new colleagues working with children who require additional support are aware of their needs?
4. How do you ensure the child and parents voice is heard at the point of transition?

THEORIES INTO PRACTICE

Though Julie Fisher's work focuses on many different aspects of practice in early childhood, the key underpinning principle is that the child is at the heart of the learning. Every pedagogical decision is made with the child in mind. When planning for your provision, your interactions, your timetables or transition, it is essential to ask the question, 'what will this be like for the child?'

By observing respectfully, taking time to reflect on your current practice and identifying strengths as well as areas for development, it's possible to manage the tension between the adult-led agenda and child-centred learning. None of this can be done in isolation. To be an effective child-centred practitioner your visions and values need to be shared with your team.

REFLECTIVE PRACTICE EXERCISE

- Does your team understand the concept of child-centred practice?
- Taking some time to reflect on your daily routine, how much of your practice is centred around the child's needs?
- Do you think you have the balance right or are there tensions?
- Is there enough time for you to interact effectively with the children?
- How might you plan to ensure that there is sufficient time for you to do so?

CONCLUSION

It has been difficult to cover Julie's extensive work into one chapter and there is so much which could have been written. This is one interpretation of her work using research literature alongside Julie's own work, which is grounded in real, practical experience with a wide range of schools and settings. Her books are accessible and offer excellent points for reflection to help leaders and teachers reflect on their current practice and give real, practical guidance on how simple changes to the way we interact with children and focus our pedagogy can have a profound and lasting impact on outcomes for children. In pedagogically challenging and turbulent times, Julie reminds us to take our focus back to the most important person, the child.

KEY QUESTIONS

How can we incorporate Julie's work on effective child-led learning into our everyday practice?

What changes can we make to ensure that the children's needs are at the heart of our decision-making processes?

How can we ensure that our interactions are respectful and lead to pedagogical flexibility, maximising the potential to develop children's learning and curiosity?

FURTHER READING

Fisher, J. (1996) *Starting from the Child*. London: Open University Press.

Fisher, J. (2016) *Interacting or Interfering*. London: Open University Press.

Fisher, J. (2020) *Moving on to Key Stage One* (2nd edn.). London: Open University Press.

Fisher, J. (2020) *Moving on to Key Stage 1: Improving Transition into Primary School* (2nd edn.). Maidenhead: Open University Press.

O'Connor, A. (2013) *Understanding Transitions in Early Years*. Abingdon: Routledge.

6

LORIS MALAGUZZI (1920–1994)

By Valerie Daniel

CHAPTER OBJECTIVES

By the end of this chapter, you will be able to:

- Recognise links to Early Childhood practice through the theory of Loris Malaguzzi.
- Understand 'the theory of the hundred languages' and children as strong, powerful learners with rights – not just needs.
- Value the environment as the third teacher.
- Apply an emergent curriculum which stems from children's experiences and interests.
- Know how to practice as a researcher using documentation as a guide to nurture children's learning.
- Explain the importance of families and community as partners in the learning process.

KEY DEFINITIONS

The image of the child	All children are seen as capable, curious, creative and able to support their own learning journeys. Working with children to explore their curiosities and interests can lead to a greater desire to learn.
Emergent curriculum	An emergent curriculum is derived from questioning and listening to the children's ideas and discussions. The curriculum 'emerges' from the children, allowing the learning process to target the development of thinking skills and children's personal learning journeys through education.

Project work	Teachers facilitate project work from children's areas of interest. Projects develop through the introduction of materials, concepts and mediums that allow children to express their ideas and interests. Projects can last anywhere from a few days to several months at a time.
Pedagogista	The 'Pedagogista' is a learning theorist whose role is to help teachers explore the thinking of children. They work closely with teacher to explore enquiry-based threads, project work and to work in partnership on best practices.
Atelierista	The 'Atelierista' has a background in education and creative arts. They challenge and support classroom teachers in introducing new concepts to children and to explore the visual possibilities of themes and projects that might not be apparent. They help teachers and children to carry out and document large project work and smaller independent activities.
Progettaziones	Progettazione is an educational approach where children and teachers are learning as collaborators and researchers and teaching each other. Progettazione includes the reflection/interpretation of pedagogical documentation and supports next steps in learning.
Environment as the third teacher	The environment is viewed as a living organism. As such, environments are thoughtfully organised to nurture creative exploration and encourage interaction and communication. Reggio classrooms are open spaces furnished with natural furnishings and natural materials, real accoutrements and natural lighting.
Documentation	Documentation serves to communicate learning and development ideas and supports the next steps in children's educational journey. Documentation may come in a variety of different forms; photography, videos, conversation transcripts, painting, drawing or other visual mediums like clay and wire.
The wider community	Learning happens anywhere, not just in school. Parents are encouraged to participate in their children's education and their daily life at school, and to extend and reinforce learning opportunities at home. Teachers are active participants in the community who work with community members.

INTRODUCTION

Early Years education is often viewed as a fluffy, rainbows and unicorns, feel-good space untouched by the harsh realities of the world. However, Early Years' theorists like Loris Malaguzzi have always been clear that the early years is not a protected bubble that insulates the sector from real life. The Early Years is very much a microcosm of our messy wider society. Loris Malaguzzi acknowledged the importance of the impact of politics in educational spaces where children lead their lives. Malaguzzi's philosophical approach was born out of the resistance movement against fascist oppression that emerged during the Second World War. Italian citizens were subject to the demands of a fascist regime under Benito Mussolini who was the Prime Minister of Italy from 1922 until his deposition in 1943. During this time the study of social sciences and any new educational theories that were based in constructivist ideals were suppressed. Whilst this chapter is not about determining the effectiveness of democratic education, it must be noted that democratic education is central to child-centred and critical pedagogies in Early Years education and, if anyone was ever in doubt of the power of education, it should be noted that apart from suppressing progressive ideas, Mussolini used the education system to indoctrinate students in fascist ideology. When the fascist regime fell at the end of the Second World War, parents were unwavering in wanting change in existing institutional practices and they longed for their children to be educated in democratic settings. Women during this time, actively sought preschool education for their children and fought to create an educational system that would raise children who could think for themselves so that fascism would never again overpower their country; these women perceived danger in an education system that nurtured children to be passive and to blindly obey.

Education at its core is inherently socio-political, and by no means a non-neutral process. It reflects the traditions, worldviews and values of the individuals who feed the systems that are responsible for educational policies and practices at national and local levels. Education exists at the intersection of social life and political life and has the power to shape cultures positively or negatively and Early Years education is no exception. As a social institution in fascist Italy, education was used to uphold and reinforce power and dominance. In 1946, Malaguzzi alongside a group of mothers started the first of many Reggio Schools with the purpose of liberating human potential as well as nurturing the development of free thinking to encourage children to become familiar with being protagonists in their own learning journeys. Freire explains that 'liberating education consists in acts of cognition, not transferrals of information' (Freire, 2005, p. 79), thereby promoting the idea that children can be active within the learning process, not passively waiting, like baby birds in a nest, to be fed knowledge from their teachers. Malaguzzi, Freire and a number of constructivist theorists at the time viewed children as powerful and capable individuals who have the capacity to construct their own knowledge and learn from their experiences. Dewey (1939), for example, emphasised that education cannot be divorced from actual life experiences, and that learning is most effective through social interactions when children are engaged in the community and the influences of their varied social and cultural environments.

Early Years education is a fascinating field that is informed by the diverse contexts that shape children's learning; these include:

- Cognitive science
- Humanistic education and social psychology
- Behavioural conditioning

These schools of thought support child development theories which focus on exploring how children change and grow socially, emotionally and cognitively over the course of their childhood. Throughout his own personal education, Malaguzzi was heavily influenced by educational theorists who espoused constructivist beliefs, although he did not necessarily agree with every aspect of their beliefs, he extracted common threads from each of their philosophical approaches and formulated three primary beliefs that inform the Reggio Emelia Approach:

- A positive image of the child
- Children learning through active participation
- Play as a vital and indispensable aspect of early learning and development

Building on the well-established theories of Dewey (1933, 1938), Erikson (1963), Piaget (1959, 1973), Vygotsky (1934, 1978) and Biber (1939, 1942, 1972), the dominant values in the Reggio Emelia Approach are focused on a child-centred, constructivist, child-led curriculum-based in experiential learning and nourished in relationship-driven learning environments.

This chapter will provide a description of Loris Malaguzzi's theory in the Reggio Emelia educational approach and how it translates into contemporary Early Years practice. The significance of political, socio-cultural and environmental influences in the field of early education will also be explored and captured in practice through the influential work of Loris Malaguzzi.

BIOGRAPHY

The Reggio Emelia Approach, renowned for being one of the most influential Early Years educational philosophies, was developed by Loris Malaguzzi who was instrumental in creating a democratic educational construct where children and teachers collaborate in the learning process. The Reggio Emelia Approach has grown consistently in popularity over the last 70 years.

Loris Malaguzzi was born in Correggio, in Northern Italy in 1920 and raised within the confines of fascism and then propelled into surviving a world at war. In 1939 at the beginning of World War II, 19-year-old Malaguzzi enrolled for a teacher training course with the encouragement of his father. During the course of the war, he completed degrees in Pedagogy and Psychology from the University of Urbino and the Italian National Research Centre in Rome. Malaguzzi was heavily affected by his life experiences, and he asserted that the war had 'gobbled up his youth' so it seems quite feasible that throughout his own education and working as a teacher in primary and secondary education during this time of oppression, that he would be drawn to and heavily influenced by educational theorists who advocated constructivism. When the war ended in 1945, Malaguzzi heard rumours of a group of women who had decided to build a school out of the wreckage left behind after the Germans retreated from Italy. The women sold German tanks, military trucks and horses and began to construct a school in a little town called Villa Cella which is a borough of Reggio Emelia. They were determined that their children would grow up as free thinkers who would fight against injustice and inequality. Malaguzzi was intrigued by this, so he rode his bike to visit this town and after speaking to these women, he was so impressed that he stayed and helped them in their venture. He is quoted as saying 'it was the women's first victory after the war because the decision was theirs. The men might have used the money differently'. Over the next 15 years the Reggio Emelia Approach began to flourish and a number of new schools were opened even though they would struggle to survive. However, in 1963, the City of Reggio Emelia responded to increased demands from its citizens to establish the first municipal preschools and in so doing, secured the sustainability of the Reggio Emelia Approach.

CONSTRUCTIVISM AND THE HUNDRED LANGUAGES

In the poem *One Hundred Languages*, Malaguzzi explains the variety of ways in which children experience the world, learn and express their learning. This poem resonates with our bodies and speaks to our minds about how we work with young children and ultimately about the image of the child in contemporary society. As practitioners, we can be restrictive and prescriptive in our work with young children or we can be open to widening the boundaries of our practice so we truly experience the variety of ways that children learn and make sense of the world. 'The hundred' is a metaphorical expression of the multiplicity and the wealth of potential in every child; our job as practitioners is to nurture and not limit this potential. The essence of the Hundred Languages is not a focus on a hundred in terms of quantity but rather about the variety of experiences, the quality of the materials and resources in the environment and the holistic approach that holds the dimensions of the image of the child, the emotional, cognitive and social needs of the child; their interests, their stories and their questions. The Hundred Languages is a key principle of the Reggio Emilia Approach to Early Childhood Education and it works on the premise that children are capable of directing their own learning (Figure 6.1).

100 languages

NO WAY. THE HUNDRED IS THERE

The child is made of one hundred.

The child has a hundred languages

a hundred hands

a hundred thoughts

a hundred ways of thinking

of playing, of speaking.

A hundred always a hundred

ways of listening

of marvelling of loving

a hundred joys

for singing and understanding

a hundred worlds to discover

a hundred worlds to invent

a hundred worlds to dream.

The child has a hundred languages

(and a hundred, hundred, hundred more)

but they steal ninety-nine.

The school and the culture separate the head from the body.

They tell the child:

to think without hands

to do without head

to listen and not to speak

to understand without joy

to love and to marvel

only at Easter and Christmas.

They tell the child:

to discover the world already there

and of the hundred they steal ninety-nine.

They tell the child:

that work and play

reality and fantasy

science and imagination

sky and earth

reason and dream

are things that do not belong together.

And thus they tell the child that the hundred is not there.

The child says:

No way. The hundred is there.

Loris Malaguzzi (translated by Lella Gandini)

Figure 6.1   One Hundred Languages

Constructivism is a teaching and learning theory that is based on the idea that learners construct knowledge through experiencing things and then reflecting on those experiences. Constructivism can be viewed as a spiral educational framework in that when learners continuously reflect on their experiences, they begin to gain knowledge that is increasing in complexity and they develop a strong ability to integrate new information with previously held knowledge. This curriculum framework captures the Reggio Emelia Approach, which focuses on collaborative learning between adults and children; formulating and testing ideas, questioning and reflecting, research and problem-solving within a learning environment that nurtures a love of learning and embraces learning as a lifelong process. As Malaguzzi explores 'Learning and teaching should not stand on opposite banks and just watch the river flow by; instead, they should embark together on a journey down the water. Through an active, reciprocal exchange, teaching can strengthen learning and how to learn' (Malaguzzi, 1998, p. 83).

Malaguzzi's enquiry-based and constructivist learning approach has links to the work of Bruner (1960) who was of the opinion that learning begins 'with the hypothesis that any subject can be taught in some intellectually honest form to any child at any stage of development' (p. 33); therefore, the concept is that even very complex material can be structured and presented in an appropriate way for the youngest children to understand by utilising a pedagogical strategy to construct concepts and consolidate understanding. Malaguzzi's Hundred Languages is essentially a conceptual model for structuring knowledge and organising learning in a way that values the uniqueness of children and their ability to be completely involved in their learning through exploring holistically with their minds, their bodies and all their senses. Psychologist, Howard Gardner theorised that maths and verbal skills are often used in the assessment of intelligence but people possess a number of other kinds of intelligences. He also explains that young children are not as yet limited by cultural patterns, social conventions and rules so they use various symbolic skills and expressive languages in a fluid manner, seamlessly moving from one field to another. Malaguzzi was also of the opinion that education is overly reliant on verbal language, to the exclusion of the multitude mediums available to learners to express themselves, including visual, musical, artistic and various other modes.

A 'SNAP-SHOT' VIEW OF THE REGGIO EMELIA APPROACH

The Reggio Emilia approach incorporates the image of the child, the environment as the third teacher, a constructed, emergent curriculum based on the interests of the child, and implements these through the ideology of multiple intelligences by way of *The Hundred Languages of Children*. We will now explore aspects of the Reggio Emelia Approach in more detail (Figure 6.2).

THE ENVIRONMENT AS THE THIRD TEACHER

Malaguzzi's philosophy regarding learning was in line with Vygotsky's belief that social learning precedes cognitive development and as such, the environment has a key role to play in the process of learning. The principle of the environment as the third teacher reflects the idea that the environment is an active participant in the educative process. According to Malaguzzi,

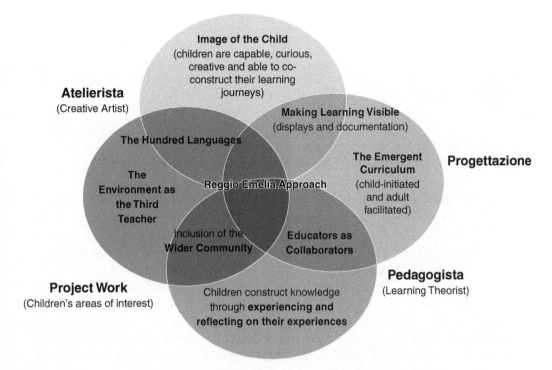

Figure 6.2 A 'snap-shot' view of the Reggio Emelia Approach

children engage with three teachers: adults, other children and the physical environment. Therefore, the environment is structured to be welcoming, aesthetically pleasing, filled with natural and purposeful materials and representative of community involvement. The physical environment in the Reggio Emelia Approach includes outdoors and indoors with these spaces being planned and organised to promote and nurture collaboration, autonomy, curiosity, communication and exploration through play, which in turn allows the environment to be shaped by the relationships and learning experiences of children and educators in partnership with families and community. Interior and exterior spaces are designed for children and adults to research and co-exist together in a flexible environment that is responsive to the creative learning journey that children undertake together with their educators. Malaguzzi (1998) employs that the environment is important and states 'It has been said that the environment should act as a kind of aquarium which reflects the ideas, ethics, attitudes and life-style of the people who live in it.'

As practitioners we put quite a bit of effort into defining best practice, but it appears that we seldom look into how our values are demonstrated in our practice and communicated through our practice. The environment as the third teacher is about how underlying values are reflected in our learning environments.

REFLECTIVE PRACTICE EXERCISE

What is the Third Teacher saying about you to your learning community? (Children, parents, staff and stakeholders).

- Are your values about children and learning evident in the environment?
  - Are children represented as active participants in their learning?
- Walk around your environment and pay attention to:
  - Lighting sources and natural light.
  - Visual clutter (Are you purposeful about what is on walls and shelves? Are books looking torn and unloved? Are rooms overcrowded with 'stuff'? How long have displays been up? Are they still relevant?) An environment that is crowded and cluttered may obscure the values you want to present.
  - Sound (Are there interesting listening experiences for children that help them to engage with their learning environment?)
  - Colour (Are the rooms painted with loud and bright colours?) Colour can often be responsible for over-stimulation in young children. Neutral colours with accent colours can support harmonious and sustained engagement with the learning environment.
- Now envisage with your team what an environment that acts as a teacher would look like, what would it feel like and what do you want it to say to your learning community.

The above is not an exercise in decorating, it is about making the values of your setting visible. Whether you intend it to or not, your environment shouts loudly about your setting's views on the child. In the Reggio Emelia Approach, the third teacher values children as capable and competent and as such the environment is flexible, well thought-out, organised and responsive to children and adults.

THE EDUCATOR'S ROLE IN DESIGNING THE ENVIRONMENT

As educators we know that an environment that supports children's growing autonomy and independence is an environment where children thrive. Children flourish in environments that invite them to be engaged in activities where they imagine, create, investigate and explore, solve problems, and make meaning from their experiences. The adult's role is to be intentional in the design and in creating the ambience of the learning environment, both indoors and outdoors and to ensure that children have time to explore. Children will engage deeply with an environment that they can relate to, so it is important to consider children, educators, families and the community in the design of the environment. Children will also maintain sustained interest in an environment that is equipped with interesting, real, hands-on, open-ended materials that reflect their interests and can be used in many ways. Classrooms in Reggio Emelia have a peaceful quality, they are uncluttered, and they prioritise opportunities for children to experiment, create, express themselves and learn. They are generally equipped with natural materials and tend to avoid plastic manufactured toys and commercially mass-produced visuals that are targeted towards the early childhood market. There is no hard or fast rule about natural materials or neutral colours, the focus is to be intentional and purposeful in the design of the environment and to give some thought to what is in the environment and how it best serves the developing child. Remember to be observant and to be playful in your learning environment. As Malaguzzi puts it 'nothing without joy'. We should never underestimate the power of joy in our learning environments. Joy comes in those wonderful moments of interaction, discovery, serendipity, exploration and play. Sprinkle joy liberally throughout the learning environment.

EMERGENT CURRICULUM

According to Gardner and Malaguzzi, it is important for Early Years practitioners to create learning environments that are stimulating for all types of learners and will support learning through children's innate interests and abilities. 'What children learn does not follow as an automatic result from what is taught, rather, it is in large part due to the children's own doing, as a consequence of their activities and our resources' (Loris Malaguzzi, 1994, *The Hundred Languages of Children*).

An emergent curriculum allows for collaboration between children and educators. Although it is generally child-initiated, it is framed by the teacher who takes on the role of facilitator. King (1993) describes the role of educators as facilitators as 'From sage on the stage to guide on the side', learners are encouraged to be proactive and involved in their learning journeys rather than passive and reactive; waiting to draw information from their teacher who is perceived as the font of all knowledge. Curriculum planning is therefore flexible, it evolves from daily life and it is constantly developing rather than written up well in advance with pre-set themes, prescribed and very limited learning outcomes for learners. A standardised curriculum often takes away the possibility of spur-of-the-moment enquiry, stealing moments of awe and wonder and reducing education to an approach where not enough attention is paid to children's differences. The emergent curriculum is dynamic and reciprocal instead of being repetitive and narrow. How can we be true to the concept of the 'unique child' as educators if we adhere to a cookie-cutter educational approach? The Reggio Emelia Approach is holistic; it involves families and communities and supports diverse cultural and linguistic heritages. In the United Kingdom, we live in a multi-cultural society, so if we consider the diversity of the children we teach, it would seem that a one size fit all, formulaic approach would be problematic.

It has to be noted that assuming the role of facilitator is not a laid-back approach to teaching; it requires educators to have the ability to adapt, to be flexible and responsive to children and also to have a clear understanding of child development and the learning process. Educators are required to use their judgements instead of rules to guide their teaching practice. Creativity and innovation are skills that serve the profession well alongside organisation and routines. This educational approach is never inflexible and never boring! It sparks surprise, it invites engagement and it is filled with joy, what more could a child ask for? In fact, what more could an educator ask for? When learning becomes more than educators actively feeding children knowledge and children passively absorbing knowledge, the process becomes a two-way relationship where educator and child have a good understanding of each other and learning becomes individualised. Educators observe deeply and they use what they see and hear to create opportunities for children to explore further, to dig deeper and to build on their knowledge. The emergent curriculum approach promotes 'learning by doing' and the cycle of listening, observing, reflecting and collaborating allows for the development of in-depth project work that can carry on over the course of weeks or months. This enquiry approach allows for covering the curriculum areas of the EYFS and also the development of important skills like critical thinking, problem solving, communication, collaboration and creativity (Figure 6.3).

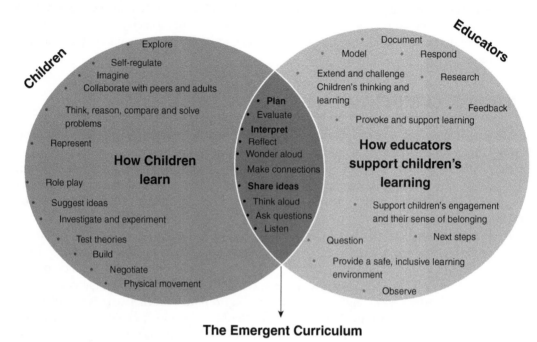

The Emergent Curriculum

Figure 6.3 The emergent curriculum: The role of children and educators within an emergent curriculum approach

The diagram above is not an exhaustive list of the roles children and educators play in the development of an emergent curriculum. In fact, it would be a good team exercise to discuss and add to the three areas.

REFLECTIVE PRACTICE EXERCISE

Are you working with a traditional curriculum in your setting? (Teacher-centred).

- Does this way of working support the unique child?
- What are the barriers to working with an emergent curriculum?
- Does your curriculum meet the needs of the individual child or is it based on standardized practice?
- Think of your setting as a doctor's surgery, discuss how standardised practice would affect patients and then apply that thinking to your setting.

EDUCATORS AS RESEARCHERS

Flexible learning environments create the scope for educators to be responsive to children's interests allowing them to use the emergent curriculum to co-construct knowledge and generate opportunities for deeper level learning. The Reggio Emelia Approach places great importance on resources, the environment, activities that provoke exploration and investigation and child and educator as co-learners and co-researchers. Nimmo and Park (2009) investigated Early Childhood Educator's professional identities and discovered educators in the Early Years were perceived as consumers of knowledge rather than creators of knowledge. This lack of value for Early Childhood Educators means that 'there is a low expectation of early childhood teachers for intellectual engagement and formal education' (p. 94). However, the Reggio Emelia approach views the educator as learner and researcher operating within the context of enquiry practices; 'We teachers must see ourselves as researchers, and to think, and to produce a true curriculum, a curriculum produced from all of the children' (Malaguzzi, 1994, p. 4).

The cycle of enquiry shown in Figure 6.4 is essentially a framework where educators and learners can scaffold the processes of planning, teaching and learning into a fluid and flexible approach which allows for the deepening of learning over time.

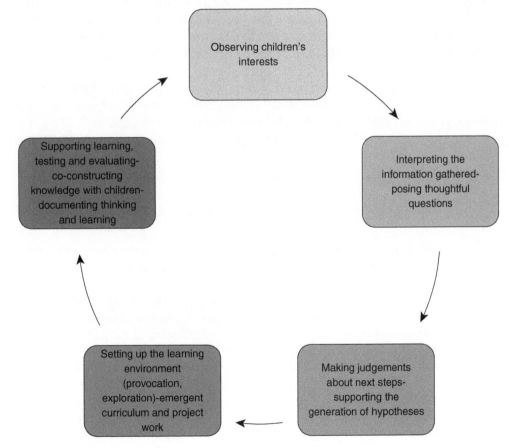

Figure 6.4 Cycle of enquiry

This way of learning focuses on the role of the child in the learning process with the role of the adult being to encourage children to be actively involved in their learning journeys through investigation and drawing conclusions. Therefore, enquiry practice requires the disposition of researchers as it involves, questioning, generating hypotheses, exploration, experimentation, interpretation, reflection and communication rendering Early Years Educators as far more than knowledge consumers and knowledge transmitters. Framing the enquiry is an important aspect of the enquiry cycle. We will now look at the case study of Reena, which explores how enquiry is demonstrated.

CASE STUDY

Reena

A child who had just come back from holidays, pointed up at the sky and spoke about going through the clouds during the plane ride and asked, 'What are clouds made of?'. In following the child's interest, Reena looked at travel and holidays and set up activities in the environment and invited me in to observe. The activities she set up undoubtedly valued the child's experience, but I asked why she had avoided the child's obvious interest in the clouds. Reena felt that clouds were too hard a concept for young children to grasp and she also did not feel that she had enough scientific knowledge about clouds. Reena was stuck in this idea of addressing clouds as a topic and she felt that travel and holidays was an easier topic to address with children. My suggestion was to spend a little time sky gazing with children. Frame the enquiry as a question – Educator – 'I wonder if we can touch clouds?' This would provoke dialogue with children, generate hypotheses, allow for further research and allow learners to receive, apply, process, retain and deepen knowledge – essentially constructing their own learning and co-constructing knowledge with the educator.

Table 6.1 is an example of questions that frame an enquiry, with the first question demonstrating process and learning/knowledge. There are two other questions from children to which you can have a go at completing with your team.

The aim of this exercise is to practice asking open-ended questions, model wondering out loud and investigating and to listen to the questions children ask and to their ideas and reflect these in exploration and investigation activities to deepen their understanding of concepts. Enquiry-based learning comes out of everyday life – out of children's natural curiosity, their interest in the world around them; rocks, trees, insects, cars, babies, food – everything! All of these interests' present opportunities for deep learning that would cover every aspect of the EYFS while embracing the natural scientist and explorer in every child. This way of working allows children to practice and develop the ability to think critically and creatively to solve problems, develop communication and language skills as they ask questions and explain their observations and conclusions and develop listening skills through collaborating with their peers and educators. Children learn to

Table 6.1 Process of learning and knowledge

Questions:	Process:	Learning/Knowledge:
Child: What are clouds made of?	**Learner hypothesis** – cotton, smoke	**Educator as co-learner and co-researcher**:
Educator: I wonder if we can touch clouds?	**Possible lines of development**:	A cloud is made of water droplets or ice crystals floating in the sky. They are formed by the reaction of water vapour to changing temperatures.
Educator: I wonder why some clouds are light and some clouds are dark?	Weather, water cycle, temperature **Experiments with adult supervision**: https:// coolscienceexperimentshq.com/ make-a-cloud-form-in-a-jar/ Experiment with boiled water, salt and string to see how evaporation works	**Child as co-learner and co-researcher**:
		Hot, cold, evaporation, steam, water cycle, weather, suitable clothes for the weather and why.
	Books:	
	Cloudy with a chance of meatballs	
	Little cloud	
	Explore my World clouds – book, YouTube	
Child: How does a worm move?		
Child: Birds come from eggs don't they? Do butterflies come from eggs?		

work as part of a team, explore their interests and develop the skills they need for further learning, for example, early literacy skills, maths skills and fine motor skills.

FAMILY AND COMMUNITY INVOLVEMENT IN THE REGGIO EMELIA APPROACH

Reggio schools were founded by families and a community that wanted a better education system for their children. They not only helped to set up Reggio schools, but they were actively involved in supporting the sustainability of these schools. This tradition continues today in schools who use the thinking behind the Reggio Emelia Approach; these schools have created an environment where dialogue between parents, educators and the wider community is integral in the way they operate. Valuing parents as co-educators acknowledges parents as an essential resource to their child's learning journey. The ongoing dialogue between parents and educators allows for a fruitful exchange of ideas which is vital in creating a constructive and productive learning environment. The needs and desires of parents are considered, and educators also support parents in being actively involved in their child's education. The families and community effort to support children's learning is dependent on cooperation and why parents are viewed as partners. Parents and community members are encouraged to volunteer in the setting as well as meet and share ideas in the piazza, look at books and resources and be involved in coffee mornings and events.

Parents and community members feel welcomed in the environment in a space that conveys harmony and pleasure in learning and parents are encouraged to integrate these ideals in their home lives as much as possible. Family and community involvement thrives on communication, information sharing and active partnership to nurture a happy and productive learning community where children are at the core.

CONCLUSION

Loris Malaguzzi is instrumental in the creation and development of the Reggio Emelia Approach and his influence has spearheaded a democratic learning process that is constantly evolving. This child-centred philosophy has international acclaim and continues to grow in popularity, but it was never Malaguzzi's aim to chase fame, he was a man who was dedicated to the development of the Reggio Emelia Approach and worked tirelessly to this end during his 39-year career and beyond; he continued to contribute to the Reggio Emelia school system even after his retirement in 1985. Loris Malaguzzi's efforts have created a long-lasting legacy that has heavily influenced Early Years education. Over 25 years after his death, the Reggio Emelia Approach, which was developed through his own trials and errors and reflective of the authenticity of co-educators and co-learners, has become a self-sustaining, evolving educational approach that is driven by the love of learning and the curiosity of children.

KEY QUESTIONS

In what ways can we use the theory of Loris Malaguzzi to enhance our work with children?

How can our settings become a little more like the principles that Loris Malaguzzi explores for our children and families?

How can we practically demonstrate our understanding of child-centred practices for our children in our settings and communities?

FURTHER READING

Smidt, S. (2017) *Introducing Malaguzzi: Exploring the Life and Work of Reggio Emilia's Founding Father.* London: Routledge.

Moss, P. (2018) *Alternative Narratives in Early Childhood: An Introduction for Students and Practitioners.* London: Routledge.

McBalain, S. (2021) *Children's Learning in Early Childhood: Learning Theories in Practice 0–7 Years.* London: SAGE Publications.

7

MARIA MONTESSORI (1870–1952)

By Sue Allingham

CHAPTER OBJECTIVES

By the end of this chapter, you will be able to:

- Recognise how the work of Maria Montessori has influenced contemporary practice and provision.
- Reflect on her theory in relation to current practices within the Early Childhood context.
- Describe the Montessori approach and practices of working with children, parents, carers and the wider social context of the family.

KEY DEFINITIONS

Casa dei Bambini	Translates as 'Children's House', and was the name of Dr Montessori's first school in Italy.
Montessori approach or method	The Montessori Method of education, developed by Dr Maria Montessori, is a child-centred educational approach based on her observations. It is an approach that values the human spirit and the development of the whole child – physical, social, emotional, cognitive.
Directress	The term used for Montessori for teachers (who were female).
Planes of development	Four periods: ages 0–6, 6–12, 12–18 and 18–24 years.
Sensitive period	A critical time for development in each of the planes.
Work	Maria Montessori described everything that children do as 'work', and believed strongly in activities and play.

INTRODUCTION

The most important period of life is not the age of university studies, but the first one, the period from birth to six.

(Montessori, 1966, p. 22)

Although many may not realise it, the thinking of Maria Montessori has had a profound effect on how we work with the youngest children today. When we reflect on her life and work with children her influence today is increasingly clear. What is also interesting are the parallels between her thinking over a hundred years ago and what is happening in Early Childhood Education today. That will be discussed at the end of the chapter.

This chapter moves from a brief biography onto how and why Montessori developed her thinking and pedagogy. The final part of the chapter reflects through case studies on how the approach is used today, how current influences have been interpreted through it, and why an understanding of Montessori is an important element of how we practice today, whether we have a Montessori setting or not. Throughout this chapter we will also explore key quotes from Montessori herself, from *The Montessori Method – Scientific Pedagogy as applied to Child Education in 'The Children's Houses'* (1912) (https://digital.library.upenn.edu/women/montessori/method/method.html#1, Accessed 13 December 2021).

BIOGRAPHY

MARIA MONTESSORI 1870–1952

Maria Montessori was very much not a woman of her time. She was a doctor who specialised in paediatrics and mental health, a rare career for a woman in those days. It was never her plan to become a teacher, which would have been a more traditional role for women this era, but her mind was changed when she had to visit children in asylums.

This was a pivotal moment, and one that still resonates today when we reflect that it is still far too common to judge children on what they are not able to do rather than what they are. In the introduction to 'The Montessori Method', referenced above, Professor Henry W. Holmes of Harvard University wrote:

It is wholly within the bounds of safe judgment to call Dr Montessori's work remarkable, novel, and important. It is remarkable, if for no other reason, because it represents the constructive effort of a woman. We have no other example of an educational system–original at least in its systematic wholeness and in its practical application–worked out and inaugurated by the feminine mind and hand.

(p. xviii)

It is interesting to note how Montessori fits into a timeline of great educational thinkers. It was an era of significance for thinking about what early teaching and learning should look like. It is no coincidence that the educational thinkers shown in Figure 7.1 still have influence today.

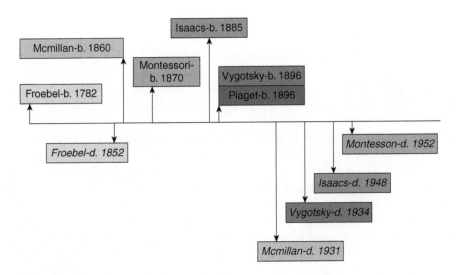

Figure 7.1   Montessori and educational thinkers

As you read through this chapter, consider how quick we often are to judge a child as being 'low ability', 'special needs' or 'disadvantaged'. These words, or labels, colour our thinking and even influence current thinking and policy about education – is this appropriate? Once we have a dominant narrative of deficit it is increasingly influential, and how is it interpreted becomes very important. It is this that struck Montessori.

As she became interested in children who did not respond to conventional schooling, she came to realise that it was not the children that had problems, rather it was the nature of the learning environment and the approaches of the teachers that were inappropriate. She learnt this after spending time observing the children, coming to the realisation that 'mental deficiency presented chiefly a pedagogical, rather than mainly a medical problem' (Montessori, 1912, p. 31).

EARLY WORK

Now one who has learned to spell mechanically all the words in his spelling-book, would be able to read in the same mechanical way the words in one of Shakespeare's plays, provided the print were sufficiently clear. He who is initiated solely into the making of the bare experiment, is like one who spells out the literal sense of the words in the spelling-book; it is on such a level that we leave the teachers if we limit their preparation to technique alone.

(Montessori, 1912, p. 12)

In this quote we see how Montessori is reflecting on the difference between a mechanistic approach to teaching and how it misses the need for an in depth and pedagogical under-standing. As we read this in the 21st century, it is interesting to reflect on how a mechanistic approach is increasingly the dominant influence in Early Childhood Education.

Her early career as a scientist meant that Montessori came to education with a different perspective. Her specialism in paediatrics meant that she had an informed viewpoint on child development and her understanding of mental health enabled her to reflect on what might trigger emotions and attitudes. When she was sent to see the children in the asylum, she realised that teaching must involve an understanding of holistic child development. She was clear 'that learning involves growth of both mind and heart through the classroom experience' (Aljabreen, 2020, p. 341).

By observing the children, Montessori realised that, to provide them with the learning and experiences that suited their needs, teaching must include the mind and the body (Montessori, 1912, p. 12).

Her belief that the best and most effective learning occurred when the senses were used led to the development of her approach. In this way, children were encouraged to feel and understand shapes, or get to know about colours, before they had to learn the technical names for them. This meant that the children had a need to find out the names, and wanted to.

Montessori was also an early advocate of what is now fashionably called 'assessment for learning' (DfES, 2003). She saw that appropriate and interesting learning would inherently reward the child, thus allowing satisfaction and good behaviour, narrow teaching and inappropriate expectations would not work in her opinion. Montessori also saw that narrow, adult led teaching gave way to children being seen as inferior and, in some way, deficient. This in turn meant that children were subjected to games and 'foolish stories.

In Chapter 2 of her 1912 book, Montessori describes how she realised through her work with the children in asylums that she was bringing them to a higher academic standard than some 'normal' children. Her understanding that children were not in any way deficient or inferior simply because they were very young (Montessori, 1933) was evident in the way she developed learning environments. For her it was very important that children had furniture, tools and resources that were suitable and that the children could use in ways that suited and satisfied them, and that they had easy access to the outdoors (Montessori, 1912, pp. 81–82). This attention to detail included a belief that all equipment and utensils should be child sized which extended to the equipment provided.

Montessori thought that early childhood teachers should:

- Provide real tools that work (sharp knives, good scissors, woodworking and cleaning tools)

  Keep materials and equipment accessible to the children, organised so they can find and put away what they need

- Create beauty and order in the classroom

(Mooney, 2000, p. 25)

Even the most formal of settings today have been influenced by the ideas of Maria Montessori. Many will not realise that, for example, that she pioneered child-sized furniture in Early Years settings.

Identifying that more could be done for the children that she saw lead Montessori to develop her approach to teaching that centred on the child. Let's look at this in more depth.

SENSITIVE PERIODS: EARLY CHILDHOOD

This chapter opened with an important quote from Montessori:

The most important period of life is not the age of university studies, but the first one, the period from birth to six.

(Montessori, 1967, p. 22)

This is significant because what she recognised as important then, we are still struggling to have acknowledged today. The early years of life are important and the learning that happens then is significant – it must be approached in an informed way.

The term 'sensitive periods' is one that is increasingly familiar to us through our continuing professional development. It is interesting to compare how Montessori described 'sensitive periods' with a contemporary commentator on neuroscience. In a paper entitled 'Sensitive Periods', Jeri Grant-Miller of the Center for Contemporary Montessori Education describes how the original concept of 'sensitive periods' was first recognised by Hugo de Vries who noticed it particularly in the lives of insects. He realised that there are 'special periods that correspond with the essential developmental stages of insects'.

(Montessori) then applied the concept of the sensitive periods to her educational philosophies. This was a unique idea in her time, as children younger than the age of six were generally regarded as incapable of receiving an education. The concept of the sensitive periods set into motion a shift in the educational philosophies of educators toward the very young children that were previously overlooked by the educational community.

(https://www.bluffviewmontessori.org/wp-content/uploads/Copy-of-Lecture-7-The-Sensitive-Periods.rtf.pdf. Accessed 26 January 2022)

Conkbayir (2021, p. 22) writes:

The concept of sensitive periods refers to distinct phases during early childhood, when the brain is best able to receive and use information gained from experience, in order to learn specific skills. The period of birth to five specifically represents a sensitive period for babies and children as it represents a time of fervent growth and development, with neural connectivity being at its most prolific.

Conkbayir goes on to point out that there needs to be consideration paid to the planning of the physical environment and resources so that a 'positive difference' can be made to the young child's ability and confidence. Particularly of note here is her comment:

That's not to say that practitioners must fit in as much teaching and learning as possible as early as possible, but to pay close attention to the layout of the environment and quality of the multi-sensorial experiences provided. Are they geared to the development of the individual child?

(Conkbayir, 2021, p. 23)

Notice the focus that both have on the child and how experiences are received by each one must be appropriate. Montessori moved on from the idea that the child was a 'mini adult' which was prevalent at the time. She turned the focus towards 'the unique qualities possessed by the young child' in order that they could be 'explored and celebrated' (Jarvis et al., 2017, p. 131).

This focus on the 'unique child' and child development is still debated today. It begs the question of why it is still not the case that we have developmentally informed Early Years practice and provision as a matter of course.

In his introduction to *The Montessori Method* (1912) Professor Henry W. Holmes notes:

The adoption of sense-training would seem to be much less a matter for variable decision. Some children may need less than others, but for all children between the ages of three and five the Montessori material will prove fascinating as well as profitable. A good deal of modern educational theory has been based on the belief that children are interested only in what has social value, social content, or "real use"; yet a day with any normal child will give ample evidence of the delight that children take in purely formal exercises. The sheer fascination of tucking cards under the edge of a rug will keep a baby happy until any ordinary supply of cards is exhausted; and the wholly sensory appeal of throwing stones into the water gives satisfaction enough to absorb for a long time the attention of older children – to say nothing of grown-ups.

(Henry W. Holmes Harvard University, 22 February 1912 https://digital.library.upenn.edu/
women/montessori/method/method.html)

Notice how this takes into account the 'fascinations' of the child and how much can be learned from these. A developmentally informed approach. In contrast here is an example from the current English Statutory Framework for the Early Years:

1.6. Educational programmes must involve activities and experiences for children, as set out under each of the areas of learning.

(DfE, 2021)

Which is heightened by this from Ofsted (2021):

Ofsted considers the curriculum as the progression model. By progress, we mean that children know more, remember more and are able to do more of what was intended in the curriculum, which is the EYFS learning and development requirements.

Inspectors will want to see that the curriculum on offer sequences the knowledge that children need. They will look at what staff teach children, and if children know and remember that curriculum.

There is no obvious room for fascinations here. Montessori saw the sensitive periods as the time when the minds of the children are at the most 'absorbent'. A progression model of teaching and learning will not enable optimum advantage to be taken of these important times.

To enable the absorbent mind, Montessori developed what we might call a constructivist approach. Whilst we may not be comfortable with the idea of constructivism in Early Childhood Education as it has overtones of linear progression and children all moving at the same rate, we must not let this influence how we read the thinking of Montessori. It's important that we avoid interpreting a historical perspective through a contemporary lens.

Her method was developed in what she called 'Planes'. And it is within the first one of these that most of the sensitive periods are situated. The idea is that recognising and understanding the sensitive periods is crucial because if one is missed or ignored, then this will have a knock on and potentially negative effect – they are interdependent. An important message is that children are unique and do not go through each period at the same time.

THE SENSITIVE PERIODS

The sensitive periods are:

- Sensitive period to language
- Sensitive period to movement
- Sensitive period to order
- Sensitive period to refinement of the senses
- Sensitive period to small details and small objects
- Sensitive period to social behaviour or to manner and courtesy

Each period works in phases depending on the child. Montessori believed that understanding this was crucial even as children get older and the 'planes' of development go into adolescence. This is an idea that we still recognise today. With this is mind, she advocated working with mixed age groups.

WHAT DOES THE THEORY LOOK LIKE IN PRACTICE?

Central to all of this is the knowledgeable and listening teacher, for which Montessori used the term 'Directress'. This is a proactive role where the adults act on what is seen and known, and the key to this is observing and using the observations:

> It is my belief that the thing which we should cultivate in our teachers is more the *spirit* than the mechanical skill of the scientist; that is, the *direction* of the *preparation* should be toward the spirit rather than toward the mechanism.

> (Montessori, 1912, p. 10)

Notice that this is more about spirit and preparation than mechanical teaching. This is a good way of understanding what is meant by 'pedagogy', a word that is often used, but less often understood. Teaching is not simply a matter of 'delivering' a predetermined programme, something that is becoming increasingly common, particularly in England under the revised Statutory Framework (2021). With reforms and revisions, it is increasingly important to reflect on the history of Early Childhood Education.

> If early education is worth studying at all, the educator who devotes his attention to it will find it necessary to define the differences in principle between the Montessori programme and other programmes, and to carry out careful tests of the results obtainable from the various systems and their feasible combinations.

> (Montessori, 1912, p. xxi)

When we look at the parallels between Montessori thinking and contemporary thinking, there is a lot that we can learn from the term 'pioneers' has been coined for these early educationalists as they pushed the boundaries and developed important ideas.

The English Statutory Framework for the Early Years Foundation Stage is based on four 'Overarching Principles':

- The unique child
- Positive relationships
- Enabling environment
- Learning and development

These four statements are effectively an equation with the first three adding together to produce the success in the final principle.

Alongside her recognition that each child is unique, the 'enabling environment' was very important to the Montessori approach. She also called it the 'favourable environment'. Underpinning it are:

- Accessibility and availability
- Freedom of movement and choice
- Personal responsibility
- Reality and nature
- Beauty and harmony

A Montessorian environment is set up in a very particular way. There will be a limited range of selected toys including building blocks. There will not be toys based on fantasy or unrealistic expectations. When we reflect on what might be seen in a present-day Early Years environment, this may seem problematic. It may even be seen to be against encouraging creativity. However, Montessori teachers disagree with this statement as they believe that the best way to nurture children's creativity is to give them contact with reality and purpose.

It is the role of the teacher to facilitate the environment to involve the children and underpin their development. This is important and something that we could usefully reflect on today. Montessori truly saw that play is the work of the child and the structure of the resources that she developed was designed to promote this.

The areas of learning she promotes are:

- Practical life
- Refinement of the senses
- Communication, language and literacy
- Numeracy and arithmetic
- Cultural aspects of life
- Creativity

Work is centred around the idea that it involves a great deal of purposeful effort and concentration and is oriented towards future achievements. Each area involves all areas of development: cognitive, emotional, social and physical.

THE MONTESSORI EARLY YEARS CURRICULUM

We must not start, for example, from any *dogmatic ideas* which we may happen to have held upon the subject of child psychology. Instead, we must proceed by a method which shall tend to *make possible to the child complete liberty*. This we must do if we are to draw from the observation of his *spontaneous manifestations* conclusions which shall lead to the establishment of a truly scientific child psychology. *It may be that such a method holds for us great surprises, unexpected possibilities.*

(Montessori, 1912, p. 30) (My own emphasis)

The word 'curriculum' is suddenly high profile in Early Years work. But it is one that really needs to be properly understood and applied in Early Childhood Education. It is a powerful word that tends to be more often thought of as applicable to more senior stages of education. Notice the words in italics above – the child is at the centre of the Montessori curriculum. That is, what is at the heart of what is taught and learnt.

In regard to infant psychology, we are more richly *endowed with prejudices* than with *actual knowledge* bearing upon the subject. We have, until the present day, wished to dominate the child through force, by the imposition of external laws, instead of making an interior conquest of the child, in order to direct him as a human soul. In this way, the children have lived beside us without being able to make us know them. But if we *cut away the artificiality* with which we have enwrapped them, and the violence through which we have foolishly thought to discipline them, they will reveal themselves to us in all the truth of child nature.

(Montessori, 1912, p. 118) (My own emphasis)

It is interesting that to get to the truth of the child, Montessori developed her thinking through observation and, like Froebel, the idea of the child in nature. But in contrast she also developed the 'materials' which, to an untrained eye, could be perceived as artificial.

The idea for these resources originally came from Edouard Seguin a French man who trained as psychiatrist. He pioneered methods for teaching the severely intellectually disabled which Montessori later adapted through experimentation and reflection.

Montessori watched children in the classroom and thought about their developmental needs; she developed materials that she thought would suit those needs; and she then watched the children with the materials, and revised and refined them until she thought she had a material that would meet one or more specific needs. So, for example, there are 10 Metal Insets, not 3 or 15, because Montessori found that different numbers did not entice the child's interest in the same way. To get the children to engage and stay engaged with the Metal Insets-and thereby develop concentration, learn to hold and handle a pencil, learn the names of the shapes, and experiment with colour and design – she found they needed 10.

(Lillard, 2008)

Take a moment to reflect on how maths is taught in Early Years in schools today. We are being led into teaching maths using a one size fits all approach. For example – all children must have an understanding of the 'ten-ness' of ten before higher numbers are addressed. But where does this leave the children who are conversant, fluent and familiar with numbers? I have often met children who would be bored and restricted by such a limited approach. We have the appearance of 'tens frames', 'subitising' and the use of 'rekenreks' as if they are a new idea, and it seems that to many they are. Those who have worked with the Montessori materials will know that her thinking and observations had already led her to creating resources. However, her use of these materials was informed by what she knew of the children and what they needed to support learning. It's worth reflecting on how we use the current resources we have and whether they are being used for and with the children, or to fulfil a predetermined model of curriculum. How are we addressing the needs and interests of the unique children through an enabling environment? Are we really proactively noticing? Are we using a pedagogical approach? I think Montessori would say that we aren't. Earlier in the chapter I noted that Montessori started as a paediatrician which gave her an insight into child development, and that she noted that children failing at school is the fault of the teaching and not the child. It is this insight into teaching and learning that underpins a truly pedagogical approach.

PEDAGOGY

THE pedagogical method of *observation* has for its base the *liberty* of the child; and *liberty is activity*.

(Montessori, 1912, p. 86)

The word 'pedagogy' is often misused in policy and practice nowadays. A pedagogical approach is one that has been carefully thought through and reflected upon.

Montessori outlined the approach she took to her teaching. She wrote:

Often the education of children consists in pouring into their intelligence the intellectual content of school programmes. And often these programmes have been compiled in the official department of education, and their use is imposed by law upon the teacher and the child.

(Montessori, 1912, p. 28)

Throughout this chapter I have noted how we are now bound by the restrictions of teaching that is being 'imposed by law'. Montessori was very clear about the principles of her approach. There are parallels with the 'Overarching Principles' of the English Statutory Framework.

The Montessori Centre International (MCI) lists the pedagogical principles of Montessori as:

- Vertical grouping
- The work cycle
- The favourable environment
- An empathetic educator

And these all underpin the idea of putting the child at the centre:

- Supporting the child as an active learner
- Respecting the inner life of the child
- Trusting the child's inner motivation

- Providing freedom within limits
- Encouraging the child's inner discipline

(https://montessori-group.com/. Accessed 14 December 2021)

MONTESSORI TODAY

Since the child now learns to move rather than to sit still, he prepares himself not for the school, but for life; for he becomes able, through habit and through practice, to perform easily and correctly the simple acts of social or community life. The discipline to which the child habituates himself here is, in its character, not limited to the school environment but extends to society.

(Montessori, 1912, p. 87)

It is interesting that the phrase about preparing children for life, and not just for school is still one that still hear today. For example, in England the Statutory Framework for the Early Years Foundation Stage (DfE, 2021) states that:

It promotes teaching and learning to ensure children's 'school readiness' and gives children the broad range of knowledge and skills that provide the right foundation for good future progress through school and life.

(DfE, 2021, p. 5)

However, there are subtle differences between the two statements as to what is meant by providing children for life:

It should be noted that for Montessori the goal of education is to allow the child's optimal development (intellectual, physical, emotional and social) to unfold. This is a very different goal to that of most education systems today, where the focus is on attainment in academic subjects such as literacy and mathematics.

(Marshall, 2017)

Throughout this chapter we have explored links between the type of work that Montessori was developing with what is happening today.

It is only right to include examples from real settings, and below are two case studies:

CASE STUDY 1: MONTESSORI PRE-SCHOOL

Montessori continues to be a role model for all early educators…

We have been established for 21 years. We were set up as a collaborative school for parents and teachers. We are run by a committee of parents and

(Continued)

(Continued)

have been lucky enough to have a very loyal and long-standing group of teachers who all been very dedicated to the school.

Every one of us has total admiration for the work of Montessori and feel it is our vocation to share that with our parents and children. We use our own Montessori curriculum with support from the app My Montessori Child which the parents have their own login for and we update daily. The EYFS is also used on the app, alongside our Montessori curriculum. The EYFS although is not our primary curriculum, the children's development is noted down in preparation for the transition to school.

The Montessori curriculum has always been aligned to the EYFS and we feel that our classrooms are able to cover the needs of the EYFS. The new EYFS has really been an easy transition for us as the new changes have been things that have been well established for us.

Our maths and literacy curriculums are comprehensive and follow the child's own learning stages, based on their Individual learning plan and not based on their age.

Our cultural materials have always ensured that the children's cultural capital is supported by giving them access to a wide range of experiences about how the world works and in-depth information about the world around them. As a charity preschool we are very conscious that Montessori has in the past had a reputation in the United Kingdom as an education system for only some children, we feel that Montessori herself wanted her education system to in be inclusive and cater for all children, especially those who were under privileged and had additional needs.

Our role as teachers is to support the children in their learning through considered observation and this is supported by the new EYFS where it is recommended that the teacher spends more time with the child playing and listening to them to see where best they can support their next steps.

We feel that the Montessori classroom with its prepared environment and the materials all available to all the children provides an enabling environment which supports the children's individual learning. At the heart of any Montessori classroom is nurturing a love of learning and helping to develop the children's confidence, this is developed through positive relationship and a feeling of community with parents.

Our day starts at 8 with early start children arriving; they are greeted and settle into their work cycle. The children then continue to arrive and we all in by 9.45. The teachers are assigned a Montessorian area to work in for that session and they will invite the children to work with them from their Individual learning plans. The children can then free flow throughout the two

(Continued)

classrooms, garden and snack area for the rest of the session. The 3-year-old plus children are invited to take part in a daily project at around 10.30 where they look more in-depth at a particular subject, for example, a continent, or life cycles or extinct animals. The children who are leaving at the morning session have a circle time which usually involves explore one of the Montessori material or a practical life lesson such a how to blow your nose.

The children who have lunch join together in a communal area to chat and eat lunch together. The children to stay all day continue after lunch for their next 3-hour work cycle. The children are encouraged to support the classrooms sense of order by mopping the floor and dusting the materials.

Montessori continues to be a role model for all early educators but we are often frustrated about the misconceptions about her work and feel that she is often under credited for her pioneering work. She was a feminist and is often not given equal status with other male Early Years educators. We are also still seen as an alternative system of learning although Montessori classrooms can be found all over the world. We are still working today with materials that have not changed in over 100 years as they still completely fulfill the purpose they were created for and have an enduring beauty.

CASE STUDY 2: MONTESSORI SETTING

Modern Montessori in a wider context…

Montessori is very compatible with many aspects of wider EY thinking, for example, Montessori has always focused on the unique learning journey of the individual child, the need for strong relationships between adults and children, the importance of the well-prepared environment, but more than this, fundamentally Montessori is about children learning through real experience, including the use of 'real' objects and resources.

The EYFS places a higher emphasis on the Prime areas, saying that where children develop well in these areas, the specific subjects will follow, and here Montessori differs – she said that where children are well stimulated intellectually, their personal skills will automatically follow, but modern Montessorians do not think that these seemingly opposing positions are irreconcilable, but instead adopt an approach whereby ALL the areas of Learning and Development are of equal importance.

(Continued)

(Continued)

> Approaches like Forest School are a perfect fit for Modern Montessorians, particularly through ideas such as confidence growing through being able to 'do' things independently and using tools safely and appropriately.
>
> Although Montessori doesn't have a very prominent health agenda, incorporating a high level of physical activity and movement into the modern Montessori day presents us with no problems or issues, in fact, the practices of yoga, Tai-Chi and mindfulness are helpful to Montessorians looking to extend children's concentration and engagement levels, by fostering a better connection between mind and body.
>
> Internationalism, cultural diversity and supporting children with EAL are all ideas highly compatible with Montessori thinking. A purely Montessori approach would not need much language to engage a child in learning aimed at the right intellectual level for them, so a lack of a shared language wouldn't prevent teaching and learning from taking place, so language development would be a separate, rather than sole focus for that child.

In summary though, my own pedagogy is to take the best of each approach and incorporate it to Montessori teaching and philosophy to create a modern, forward thinking and adaptive Montessori practice. I believe that children can have the best of ALL worlds – amazing play opportunities, quality interactions with skilled practitioners (who I still call teachers!) and specific adult led 'teaching' based on the interests and developmental strengths and areas for development of the individual child. Overall, in our setting, this leads to a very high level of engagement and therefore very positive behaviour!

What I should have added is the idea of intrinsic motivation – this theme runs across Forest School, Curiosity Approach and Montessori, and makes them all compatible with each other!

Montessori did her substantive theoretical work at the very beginning of the 20th century. As we consider and try to implement her method of education at the very beginning of the 21st century, it would be foolish indeed to treat Montessori's concepts of childhood, learning and development (or 'Montessori philosophy', as many of her contemporary adherent's term these things) as if they should not be modified substantially in the light of the growth of knowledge about children over the century in question.

CONCLUSION

The interpretations of Montessori's work are interesting to note in the light of this chapter because three things have happened:

- Montessori's ideas are used so habitually that their origins are often not realised or acknowledged.
- The Montessori name can be applied to any setting as a marketing ploy or simply out of naivete, but what actually happens within may bear little resemblance to Montessori theory or practice.
- 'Purist' Montessori settings run by trained staff can find it difficult to meet the statutory expectations of the Early Years Foundation Stage Curriculum, particularly about the teaching of early reading and writing. This can be met with criticism.

The case studies shared here from the two modern-day Montessorians show just how the influence of her theories can be used in different ways that remain fundamentally faithful to the principles. Reflecting on the thinking of Maria Montessori is interesting in the current climate of prescribed curriculum and testing. We can learn a lot.

MONTESSORI'S KEY CONTRIBUTIONS

- A narrow, imposed curriculum does not lead to effective learning. There is a danger that children can be seen as deficient, whereas it is the curriculum that doesn't meet their needs.
- Close observation of a child is key to finding out the learning needs.
- The environment, both physical and emotional, inside and out, must be appropriate and set up so that the children can be independent and not held back or restricted. They must be able to explore.

It seems only appropriate to give the last word to Montessori and hold her thoughts as we consider our practice and provision today:

> To-day we hold the pupils in school, restricted by those instruments so degrading to body and spirit, the desk–and material prizes and punishments. Our aim in all this is to reduce them to the discipline of immobility and silence, – to lead them,– where? Far too often toward no definite end.

> Often the education of children consists in pouring into their intelligence the intellectual content of school programmes. And often these programmes have been compiled in the official department of education, and their use is imposed by law upon the teacher and the child.

> Ah, before such dense and wilful disregard of the life, which is growing within these children, we should hide our heads in shame and cover our guilty faces with our hands!

> (Montessori, 1912, p. 27)

KEY QUESTIONS

In what ways can you use Maria Montessori methods to enhance your work
  with children?
What can Early Childhood settings take from her theory for our children and
  families?
How can we practically demonstrate our Early Childhood pedagogies in our
  communities?

FURTHER READING

Sharma, A. and **Cockerel, H.** (2014) *Mary Sheridan's From Birth to Five Years: Children's Developmental Progress* (4th edn.). London: Routledge.

Conkbayir, M. and **Pascal, C.** (2014) *Early Childhood Theories and Contemporary Issues: An Introduction.* London: Bloomsbury Academic.

8

TINA BRUCE

By Philippa Thompson

CHAPTER OBJECTIVES

By the end of this chapter, you will be able to:

- Recognise the links to Early Childhood practice through the theoretical perspectives of Tina Bruce.
- Consider the 12 features of play from the perspective of Tina Bruce and understand the complexities of defining play.
- Describe the influence of Froebelian principles on the work of Tina Bruce.
- Know how to apply the ten principles of early childhood to early childhood practice.
- Consider the importance of recognising the contribution, diversity and individuality of families.
- Explain how a holistic approach to early childhood education supports young children and their families.
- Consider the importance of highly skilled practitioners and the policy context.

KEY DEFINITIONS

Play	This is complex to define. Bruce suggests that play is seen through differing lenses dependent on the philosophical basis of the educator. Her 12 features of play will be explored in this chapter.
Froebel	Friedrich Froebel (1782–1852) created the first kindergarten in 1836 for children under the age of seven. He focused on education through enquiry, with children as active rather than passive learners. His key principles included having play at the centre; being engaged with nature and a holistic approach to early education. He also placed emphasis on creativity and the key role of the knowledgeable adult.

Holistic	Bruce considers the Froebelian principle that there is a 'connectedness' between children and their environment. Her educational perspective is that practitioners need to consider education and the child as a whole entity. Learning in a holistic way means that the whole child is connected with their learning and that this should not be fragmented into subject areas.
'Schoolification'	As the importance of early childhood has been recognised by successive governments in England, so has the increase in policy directing practice. It is argued that this directive style of policy has caused early childhood practice to become more formalised with an emphasis on adult-led practice. This style of practice is not supported by contemporary research and that of Bruce.
Neoliberalism	Over the past 40 years and successive governments, the United Kingdom has followed a political ideology called neoliberalism. In early childhood this has positioned parents as consumers and children as future investments; encourages market competition (the growth of private day care); standardised curriculum and it is argued a 'top down' pressure to address standards.
Childhood	Bruce suggests that childhood is not a time to prepare children for future learning. She promotes the strongly researched philosophy that children are unique in their learning style and are learners from birth.

INTRODUCTION

Many of you will be familiar with the name Tina Bruce as she is an author with considerable impact. This is often due to the accessible nature of her writing and presentation. However, you may not be aware of the wide-ranging influence of her work on practice in early childhood, which this chapter will explore. It is not possible to cover all her work within the scope of this chapter, and therefore key aspects have been selected so that you can become familiar with her work. This will hopefully encourage you to find out more using the further reading suggestions at the end.

Tina Bruce is perhaps most well known for her development of the ten principles of early childhood linked closely to Froebelian principles in 1987. However, there are other equally important contributions to early childhood education that need highlighting. This chapter seeks to uncover some of her key works and support your understanding of the contribution this has made to research and practice.

The chapter provides a short synopsis of the following key elements of Bruce's work:

- play, early education and the ten principles
- the influence of Froebel on her work and on contemporary practice
- the influence of her work on your own philosophy and practice
- the political context in England
- advocating for the need for highly skilled practitioners in early education
- the 12 features of play
- the importance of creativity at the heart of early childhood
- recognising the contribution, diversity and individuality of families

BIOGRAPHY

Professor Tina Bruce CBE is a recognised researcher and author within the field of early childhood education. She initially trained as a primary teacher at the Froebel Educational Institute, now part of University of Roehampton, where one of her tutors was Chris Athey. Froebel was and continues to be her inspiration. She has worked with the British Council in Egypt and New Zealand, with British schools in China and Egypt and since 2005 has been involved in a family and community project in South Africa. In 2008, Tina Bruce was awarded a CBE for services to Early Years education which recognised her contribution through research literature and teaching. She also spent ten years coordinating the Early Years Advisory Group for successive UK government ministers. Tina Bruce is most widely known for her ten principles of early childhood and her 12 features of play which are used by many to make links between theory and practice. Her work is well known for being accessible to a wide range of readers which in turn creates impact. It has resulted in two Lifetime Achievement awards in recognition of her continuing contribution to early childhood. Bruce has written over 30 books as well as articles and many conference presentations. Her passion for the subject area makes her an engaging speaker, and she continues to be engaged with current research and practice.

TEN PRINCIPLES OF EARLY CHILDHOOD EDUCATION

Many early childhood degree students and practitioners will be familiar with Bruce's ten principles. These stand the test of time and are still relevant today. They demonstrate Bruce's commitment to quality practice in early childhood. An important aspect of her work is its accessibility for all levels of practitioner and students. Each of the ten principles provides elements for critical discussion in the lecture hall alongside the staff room. Her research has had a significant impact on practice due to this accessibility.

The principles are set out below and reflect the key elements of Bruce's writing over time which focus on the idea of a holistic approach; child-initiated play; self-discipline and the importance of community. Later in this chapter there will be an opportunity for you to reflect on your own practice experience against these principles and consider how you could improve your own understanding. Bruce considered the ten principles as:

1. Childhood is seen as valid in itself, as part of life and not simply as preparation for adulthood. Thus, education is seen similarly as something of the present and not just preparation and training for later.
2. The whole child is considered to be important. Health – physical and mental – is emphasised, as well as the importance of feelings and thinking and spiritual aspects.
3. Learning is not compartmentalised, for everything links.
4. Intrinsic motivation, resulting in child-initiated, self-directed activity, is valued.
5. Self-discipline is emphasised.
6. There are specially receptive periods of learning at different stages of development.
7. What children can do (rather than what they cannot do) is the starting point in the child's education.
8. There is an inner life in the child, which emerges especially under favourable conditions.

9. The people (both adults and children) with whom the child interacts are of central importance.
10. Quality education is about three things: the child, the context in which learning takes place, and the knowledge and understanding which the child develops and learns.

(Bruce, 1987; 2015)

THE INFLUENCE OF FROEBEL

Tina Bruce trained at the Froebel Education Institute and the influence of Froebelian principles is a key part of her philosophy and work. She writes about the relevancy of his work today but also how it should continue to grow and develop with changes in society. She has written widely about the influence of Froebel's theories and principles on her own work. A keen advocate of his philosophy of education, Bruce's writing is influenced by Froebel's ideas of the unique child, unity and connectedness and the importance of play as central to education (Manning, 2005).

The idea of a credit rather than a deficit model, starting from what children know and can do is strongly advocated by Bruce as a quality early childhood approach. This sees the work of Froebel being related to more contemporary international approaches such as Te Whariki (Carr, 2006). Connections can also be made to more recent funds of knowledge research that consider the impact of practitioners understanding the knowledge children bring from home (Chesworth, 2016; Hedges, Cullen and Jordan, 2011). Bruce is very clear in her writing that it is important for Froebelian principles to remain contemporary and relevant. Her work continues to reflect this as she embraces change while staying true to her beliefs and passion for early childhood practice.

It is clear that Froebel provides Bruce with a strong influence to which she refers and uses to develop her own thinking and research. Knowing what your beliefs are and understanding your underpinning philosophy will help you to develop your own practice that can remain consistent. Try using the reflection questions below to consider your own philosophy and principles.

REFLECTIVE PRACTICE EXERCISE

Whose work has influenced your thinking in the following areas:

- How do you believe children learn?
- What theoretical perspectives do you base this belief on?
- When you observe children's play what do you look for?
- What does parent partnership mean to you in practice?

You may have your passion about early childhood practice, just as Tina Bruce has developed hers, but in many countries, practice comes under the scrutiny of government. This sometimes can result in a clash of ideologies. Tina Bruce has managed to maintain a strong identity of principles while still influencing practice in a changing political climate. The next part of this chapter explains the political context that Bruce's work has continued to develop within.

THE POLITICAL CONTEXT

Bruce's research began at a time prior to the Education Reform Act in 1988. At the time teacher education and early childhood were thriving, with nursery schools led by head teachers, qualified teachers and Level 3 practitioners. Trainee teachers were supported to understand how children learn from a critical and practical perspective alongside four years degree study.

In 1988 however, it became clear that the UK Government were concerned with data suggesting that there were still children not at an expected standard for their reading, writing and mathematical ability (Wyse and Torrance, 2009). The National Curriculum (1989) was designed to address this, with a strong focus on standards. Education in the classroom would no longer be fully the domain of the teacher.

However, Bruce continued to advocate for the importance of play and that early childhood practitioners needed to be knowledgeable about play. This important work continued in a difficult climate as in 1997 the emphasis became stronger in terms of assessment and monitoring of standards. The appearance of a 'top down' pressure on early childhood practitioners to have a more formal style of practice in Reception and nursery classes became a reality. 'Schoolification' became a subject explored in research as practitioners and researchers raised concerns about being too formal too soon in England. Bruce's work on the importance of play has continued to resonate with practitioners and students. It has become increasingly important that those working with young children in England have a deep understanding of child-initiated play to position themselves as advocates for play. If this knowledge is not developed and continued, then children's well-being could be at risk. While neoliberalist principles link the economy to education and markets that compete over standards, it is also vital that early childhood has knowledgeable and well-qualified practitioners.

In her most recent work, Bruce (2021) considers the key themes and debates involved within a Froebelian approach. One of the aspects that Bruce champions is the need for highly skilled practitioners. She has been an advocate of this for many years as the UK government has not committed to a clear qualification strategy or a graduate workforce. Practitioners that know and understand how children are intrinsically motivated to play and how best to support this continues to be a key feature of her work.

SUPPORTING A HIGHLY SKILLED WORKFORCE

In 2020, Birth to Five Matters was developed by members of a newly developed Early Years coalition which brought together a wide representational body of the sector. The coalition produced non-statutory guidance for practitioners to use to support the implementation of an updated Statutory Framework for the Early Years Foundation Stage. This was as a direct response to what was considered to be another attempt at formalising curriculum for children 0–5 years old. Bruce's contribution to Birth to Five Matters involved a section encouraging practitioners to engage with nature across early childhood. Here she combined her passion to continue to support practitioners who can think for themselves and have strong pedagogical beliefs alongside Froebel's belief of an understanding of nature as central to a child's education (Bruce, 2012). While there is not scope to fully explore Bruce's passion for nature and connectedness to the universe, this next reflective exercise is a starting point for your own thinking.

REFLECTIVE PRACTICE EXERCISE

Consider how your outdoor play area reflects how children are enabled to engage with nature:

- From a baby's perspective?
- From a young child's perspective?
- From a parent's perspective?
- From staff members' perspectives?
- From a leaders/manager's perspective?

The above exercise should help you to consider whether children in your setting are engaging with nature when they are outdoors or whether your outdoor space is simply perceived as a place where children 'let off steam'. Further considerations could be:

- How long do the children in your setting spend outside? Do they have time to 'wallow' in their play?
- Who decides when the children go outside and how long they spend outside?
- Does your environment reflect individuality, diversity and equality?

This next part of the chapter returns to play as a crucial element of Tina Bruce's work. Here it is acknowledged that play is not easy but that it has much to offer children, their families and highly skilled practitioners.

PLAY: COMPLEX AND PROBLEMATIC

Play is central to Bruce's work but it is complex and problematic, and as Bruce (2013, p. 129) suggests, 'there is widespread confusion about what it is'. For those who seek to try and measure children's progress through data, it poses numerous difficulties and therefore in some Reception classes in particular play becomes a problem to those who do not understand it. Bruce (2001) suggests that play enables children to use what they already know to develop their learning in creative and flexible ways. Her work is key to highlight the need for a deep understanding of play. Bruce's 12 features of play enable those studying and in practice to consider their own understanding.

TWELVE FEATURES OF PLAY

As mentioned earlier in the chapter, there are 12 features of play identified and developed by Bruce. She reflects on these on the Froebel Trust website (https://www.froebel.org.uk/. Accessed 13 December 2021) in March 2020:

1. *Free flow play actively uses direct, first-hand experiences, which draw on the child's powerful inner drive to struggle, manipulate materials, explore, discover and practise over and over again.*

2. *Play exerts no external pressure on children to conform to externally imposed rules, goals, tasks or a definite direction. In this it differs from games. But the externally set rules in games enable children to experiment with breaking, making and keeping rules in the safety of their free-flowing play.*

3. *Play is an active process without an end product. When the play fades, so does its tangibility. It can never again be replayed in exactly the same way. It is of the moment and vanishes when the play episode ends. This aids flexibility of thought and the adaptability central to the intellectual life of the child.*

4. *Play is intrinsically motivated. It does not rely on external rewards. It is self-propelling. Children cannot be made to play. The circumstances and relationships need to be right for the child's play to begin to flow.*

5. *Play is about possible, alternative, imagined worlds which involve 'supposing' and 'as if' situations. These lift participants from the literal and real to a more abstract and higher level of functioning. This involves being imaginative, creative, original and innovative. The symbolic life of the child uses life experiences in increasingly abstract ways.*

6. *Play is sustained, and when in full flow, helps children to function in advance of what they can actually do in their real lives. They can drive a car, perform a heart operation, be a shop keeper.*

7. *Play can be initiated by a child or an adult, but if by an adult he/she must pay particular attention that the adult's play agenda is not the most important or only one. Free-flowing play is more like a conversation with each listening to and tuning into the other.*

8. *Play can be solitary and gives children agency and a sense of control over their lives. It supports children in developing awareness and strength in their own ideas, feelings and relationships. It gives personal space for contemplation and well-being because it gives strength to deal with life's events.*

9. *Play might be in partnerships between children or between adult and child. Or it might be in a group with or without an adult participating. Adults need to be sensitive to children's play ideas, feelings and relationships and not invade, overwhelm or extinguish the children's possibilities for free-flowing play. Freedom with guidance is a delicate balance.*

10. *Play is about wallowing in ideas, feelings and relationships and the prowess of the physical body. It helps the process of becoming aware of self in relation to others and the universe. It brings unity and interconnectedness.*

11. *During their free-flowing play children use the technical prowess, mastery and competence they have developed to date. They are confident and in control. Play shows adults what children already know and have already learnt more than it introduces new learning.*

12. *Play is an integrating mechanism which brings together everything the child has been learning, knows and understands. It is rooted in real experience that it processes and explores. It is self-healing in most situations and brings an intellectual life that is self-aware, connected to others, community and the world beyond. Early childhood play becomes a powerful resource for life both in the present and the future.*

The above 12 features also illustrate the complexity and depth of play. It is not simply an exercise of putting resources out for children and letting them play. Equally Bruce also discusses that highly skilled practitioners know when children should be left and observed in their play and when to intervene to support play further. There are also key aspects of play that Bruce's work highlights as essential parts of play and we go on to consider those next.

PLAY, INCLUSION AND CREATIVITY

Play and creativity for Bruce are entangled and by their very nature can be inclusive. The idea that play is intrinsically motivated and comes from within the child is an important element. The quality of the play will depend on previous experiences. Bruce again is influenced by the work of Froebel who considered children as whole beings interconnected to the universe around them. Bruce advocates for child-initiated play and the importance of an inclusive environment. She is clear that the play experience will be much more significant if children feel more comfortable in their play environment and, for example, can play in their home language (Bruce, 2013).

'WALLOWING IN PLAY'

Bruce is synonymous with the concept of wallowing:

We can express the essence of the features of free flow play through this equation:

Free flow play = wallow in ideas, feeling, and relationships + the application of competence, mastery and control already developed.

(Bruce, 2003, p. 21)

Much of her writing considers the aspect of young children having time to play and in fact named one of her books after this in 1991. The idea that if children have time to become engaged and 'wallow' in their play without interruptions from adults or routine, this then enables them to think and explore their own learning. Flexibility of thought and experimentation need time and time alone for some children. Bruce (2013, p. 156) suggests that 'solitary play engages children in the deepest levels of thought and idea creation...'

The importance of time and space in order for children to wallow in their play is strongly associated with Bruce. Both historical and more contemporary research aligns with this idea of being immersed in play. Csikszentmihalyi (1996) refers to the state of 'flow' in children's play which is often reflected upon in outdoor learning. Ferre Laevers (2000) has worked with practitioners on the impact of the environment on a child's level of involvement. The idea of wallowing connects closely to 'flow' and 'involvement', and further reading will enable you to understand the subtle differences and similarities of this work.

CASE STUDY

Tom, 4 years and 6 months when he starts school in England

Tom has started in Reception and is an active four-year-old. His parents have noticed that he enjoys 'wallowing' in his play at home and this has also been noted by his childminder. Her favourite phrase was 'Tom, time to come back in the room' as sometimes he was so engaged in solitary play that he noticed nothing else around him. His childminder, parents and preschool encourage this love of exploration and enquiry through creative and physical play experiences. They are knowledgeable practitioners and understand about schema in play. They support Tom's interests in trajectory and enveloping schema through some large-scale sensory painting experiences. His parents also encourage him to use his whole body when using creative materials such as paint.

Tom returns home a few weeks into school and says, 'I don't like painting anymore mummy. They make me sit down and tell me what to paint'.

The above case study provides some examples of Bruce's principles previously mentioned. Are you able to see them in the practice described? Reflecting on these and the case study, think about your own practice and the practice you have witnessed using the reflection points below:

REFLECTIVE PRACTICE EXERCISE

- Are you able to see the difference in practice between home, childminder, preschool and school?
- What Froebelian principles can you identify here?
- Why do you think this has happened?

The next section will consider how Bruce focuses her work on engaging with families and how this should be approached. There are many examples of working in partnership in a range of settings, but have you ever considered what your philosophy is and how you really think about working with families?

WORKING WITH FAMILIES

A key message from Bruce is that when working with children, families and the community, they should not ever be perceived as deficient. The idea of the family and practitioners as a strong team is essential to Bruce and that a Froebelian approach involves the family being supported to parent the child in a way that suits them and that they have the support of the community. Again, this refers back to Bruce's belief that practitioners working with young children require expertise and a deep level of knowledge. It is not just the child they are working with but the child as part of a wider community. Bruce writes about the entanglement of environment, people and culture all having an impact on children's learning.

A recent addition to Bruce's work in communities is based in practice in Soweto, South Africa. In 2005, Bruce responded to an invitation from the Kliptown community where she has developed and supported the embedding of Froebelian pedagogy into early childhood practice. Her writing confirms that this has not been without ethical dilemmas about cultural inappropriateness and thoughts of colonialism. Ethical practice has been central to the project alongside a true partnership with the community. Listening to the needs and desires of a community again requires skilled and empathetic practitioners who understand the benefits to young children of working together.

Bruce and her team stayed true to her Froebelian principles of unity which meant addressing the significant child welfare needs alongside quality early childhood teacher training. Bruce's influence and previous research can be clearly identified in the approach to this project and as a significant contributor to its success. Supporting young children to become confident, independent, playful and creative free thinkers is the essence of Bruce's work. Embracing local communities and traditions as part of an holistic approach to early childhood education had positive outcomes for children, practitioners and families (Read, 2018). This is a project that encompasses the positivity and depth of knowledge that Bruce has contributed over many years to the discipline of early childhood.

After considering the work of Tina Bruce with families, you can now consider how this might impact on your practice. Bruce is considered an advocate for quality practice, and by training others it is hoped that practitioners will continue to understand the benefits of play, unity, connectedness and an holistic approach. Having looked at some of the key aspects of her work, it is time to consider your own role and responsibilities in advocating for quality practice to continue. The reflective practice exercise may challenge you to think more deeply about your practice, and it is important to remember that your perspectives may change and evolve over time. The second activity using the grid is to support you to develop your ideas around practice even further using Bruce's work to support your thinking.

REFLECTIVE PRACTICE EXERCISE: ADVOCATING FOR QUALITY PRACTICE

As a professional within early childhood, how do you advocate for play in your setting?

- How are you relating your practice to the ten principles of early childhood?
- Have you managed to reflect on why child-initiated play is important? Are you able to discuss child-initiated play with your colleagues?

(Continued)

(Continued)

- How does everyone in your setting feel play is valued by the children, families and other professionals?
- Think about your role currently. How do you make sure that the individual child's play is supported and how you can improve this further?

Using the grid below, consider the Ten Principles of Early Childhood in relation to your own practice/placement experience (Table 8.1).

Table 8.1   Applying the ten principles to your practice

Principle	Where do you see examples of this principle in your current practice?	How could you support the development of this principle in your future practice?	How could you change your environment to support the development of these principles?
Childhood is seen as valid in itself, as part of life and not simply as preparation for adulthood. Thus, education is seen similarly as something of the present and not just pre-paration and training for later.			
The whole child is considered to be important. Health – physical and mental – is emphasised, as well as the importance of feelings and thinking and spiritual aspects.			
Learning is not compart-mentalised, for everything links.			
Intrinsic motivation, resulting in child-initiated, self-directed activity, is valued.			
Self-discipline is emphasised.			
There are specially receptive periods of learning at different stages of development.			
What children can do (rather than what they cannot do) is the starting point in the child's education.			

(Continued)

Table 8.1   Applying the ten principles to your practice   (Continued)

Principle	Where do you see examples of this principle in your current practice?	How could you support the development of this principle in your future practice?	How could you change your environment to support the development of these principles?
There is an inner life in the child, which emerges especially under favourable conditions.			
The people (both adults and children) with whom the child interacts are of central importance.			
Quality education is about three things: the child, the context in which learning takes place, and the knowledge and understanding which the child develops and learns.			

CONCLUSION

It has been difficult to place all of the many years of Tina Bruce's work into one chapter, and there is so much more that could have been written about. This is one interpretation of her work using research literature to support and the work of Bruce herself. Achieving two lifetime achievement awards suggests how valued she is within the sector. Her work remains accessible to all through her style of writing and her engagement with practitioners. She continues to work tirelessly and her passion for Froebel is clear. The idea of moving the work of Froebel into contemporary times and making it relevant for a range of communities is testament to her considerable knowledge and adaptability. Her impact on early childhood play is significant through her twelve features of play which encompass the meaning of play while remaining accessible. The principles of early childhood will hopefully continue to shape quality practice for many years regardless of political landscapes. Children are unique and deserve their educators to understand so that they can become the confident, self-directed creative thinkers of tomorrow.

KEY QUESTIONS

In what ways can we use the principles theory to enhance our work with children?

How can our settings become part of the solution for our children and families?

How can we practically demonstrate our loving pedagogy in our communities?

FURTHER READING

Bruce, T. (1991) *Time to Play in Early Childhood Education*. London: Hodder and Stoughton.

Bruce, T. (2020) *Educating Young Children: A Lifetime Journey into a Froebelian Approach: The Selected Works of Tina Bruce*. Abingdon: Routledge.

Bruce, T. (2021) *Friedrich Froebel: A Critical Introduction to Key Themes and Debates*. London: Bloomsbury.

Bruce, T., Elfer, P. and Powell, S. (eds) (2019) *The Routledge International Handbook of Froebel and Early Childhood Practice: Re-articulating Research and Policy*.

Louis, S., Bruce, T. and Bruce I. (2021) Teacher Progression in a South African Community School in an Informal Settlement. *IMPACT*, 11, 25–28.

Palmer, A. and Read, J. (eds) (2021) *British Froebelian Women From the Mid-Nineteenth to the Twentieth Century: A Community of Progressive Educators*. Abingdon: Routledge.

Read, J. (2018) Taking Froebel abroad: Transnational travel by Froebelian teachers in the 1910 and 2010s: India and South Africa. *An International Research Journal*, 34(6), 387–392.

9

VALERIE DANIEL

By Aaron Bradbury

CHAPTER OBJECTIVES

By the end of this chapter, you will be able to:

* Recognise the links to Early Childhood Practice through the research of Daniel by discussing leadership and management, anti-racist discourses in the Early Childhood Education and Care (ECEC) sector.
* Define the pioneering work of equality, diversity and inclusion and how this is embedded into Early Childhood practice.
* Describe the practices of working with children, families and professionals through safe spaces.
* Explain the importance of equality, diversity and inclusive nurturing care for all children in the Early Years.

KEY DEFINITIONS

Equality	Equality is about ensuring that every individual has an equal opportunity to make the most of their lives and talents.
	It is also the belief that no one should have poorer life chances because of the way they were born, where they come from, what they believe or whether they have a disability.
	Equality recognises that historically certain groups of people with protected characteristics such as race, disability, sex and sexual orientation have experienced discrimination.

Diversity	Diversity means having a range of people with various racial, ethnic, socioeconomic and cultural backgrounds and various lifestyles, experience, and interests. ... An equal representation of age, race, gender, socioeconomic status, religion and political perspectives in the patient population.
Inclusion	Inclusion means that every child has access to, participates meaningfully in, and experiences positive outcomes from Early Childhood education and care programs. Inclusion resources are an important part of how we support high-quality Early Childhood education and care.
Anti-racist practice	Anti-racism is a process of actively identifying and opposing racism. The goal of anti-racism is to challenge racism and actively change the policies, behaviours and beliefs that perpetuate racist ideas and actions.
Leadership	Leadership involves having a mature understanding of children, families and communities. Whereas effective leadership consists of higher knowledge, skills which vary in those who are needed for the provision of education and care (Moyles and Yates, 2004).
Management	An Early Year's manager plays a crucial role in an Early Years setting, and they are one of the most influential people in any Early Years setting. They create policies, procedures, manage practitioners, deal with parents, manage accounts and ensure everyone is doing their best for the children.
Pedagogy	Pedagogy is about how we educate children and help their development. It's the techniques and strategies you can use to provide opportunities for development and how your relationships and interactions with children can affect them.
Anti-oppressive practice	Means giving up power, being inclusive of all groups, of all marginalised groups, having representation from these groups and having joint decision-making about policy, procedures and practices.
Absolutism	The political doctrine and practice of unlimited centralised authority and absolute sovereignty, as vested especially in a monarch or dictator.

INTRODUCTION

It is important that we give credibility to some of the contemporary people who are leading the way within Early Childhood, and Dr Valerie Daniel is no exception. You may have heard about her from her day-to-day practices as a Maintained Nursery School Headteacher, but if you look a little deeper you will know that she has conducted extensive research, written a comprehensive thesis and has spoken with poise, knowledge and rigour when it comes to the Early Childhood sector. She speaks about leading the way on many contemporary issues, including:

* Leadership and management
* Anti-racist practice
* Equality, diversity and inclusion

Research and current trends show us that the pioneering work that Daniel has done within the sector is one in which we need to advocate for the unique child and for professionals to continue their focus on the child.

Inclusive practices and equalities are an important factor within our day-to-day role. It comes with a commitment to valuing and respecting the diversity of an individual. Children, families and the whole community must sit at the heart of Early Childhood practices. We can't get away from the inequalities within society, which has a far-reaching effect on children's development, education, health and life chances. As stated in the Birth to Five Matters Guidance, 'settings have a vital role to play in explicitly addressing all forms of discrimination and prejudices' (2021, p. 24).

It goes without saying that by doing this as a professional and within the context of the setting you can meet the Equality Act 2010 and the requirement that no child or family is discriminated against in terms of their protected characteristics, outlined in the diagram below (Figure 9.1):

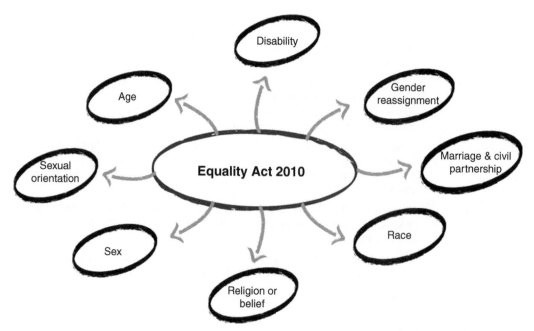

Figure 9.1   Equality act 2010 – characteristics

Within her work, Daniel encompasses the Equality Act 2010 through many of her applications to anti-oppressive practices. You could argue that this is embedded and runs through all of her discussions. She believes that anti-oppression shouldn't become a silo and it ivs important when promoting an anti-oppressive approach within the Early Years, we do so with the Equality Act 2010 at the heart of that practice.

BIOGRAPHY

Dr Valerie Daniel is a recognised authority within the field of Early Years practice and child development. Born and raised in Jamaica, Dr Valerie Daniel is a qualified teacher with over 30 years' experience with the last 14 years in the role of a Maintained Nursery School headteacher. Valerie is a Doctor of Education (University of Birmingham) and a trained systems leader and leadership mentor for other headteachers and leaders in the Early Years sector. She has a deep interest in the dynamics of the current Early Years sector and wrote her doctoral thesis on 'The Perceptions of a Leadership Crisis in the Early Years Sector'. This research fostered a deep interest in how crises develop and how to effect change in these circumstances. Valerie proposes that the current issues around systemic racism and all forms of oppression and discrimination have the hallmarks of a crisis that has deep roots in deeply dysfunctional public systems that do not value people equally and rely on a divided nation remaining divided.

Valerie started her research journey at Birmingham University and became a Doctor of Education in 2019. Valerie's research not only sparked a discussion within the sector with regards to the leadership and policies surrounding it, but also highlighted the need for it to become more accessible and advocated for more of a focus on a leadership crisis within the Early Years sector. This research critiqued the landscape of current ideology around Early Years education in its widest forms, including key aspects of privatisation of the Early Years. From this Dr Valerie Daniel gained a voice, one in which she was able to use to make change and pioneer work within leadership and management, whilst focusing heavily on equality, diversity and inclusion. Speaking at high profile conferences and practice-led discussions, Valerie was able to discuss equality, diversity and inclusion, focusing on anti-racism, and by doing so has begun a chain reaction of debate, critique and further dialogue for the sector. It is this aspect of her work which has become a pioneering voice for the sector and the focus of this chapter.

ANTI-OPPRESSIVE PRACTICES IN EARLY CHILDHOOD

Anti-oppressive practices apply to all children, families and colleagues. To truly think about this, 'each characteristic of identity needs to be applied to all people, not just those within minoritized groups' (Birth to Five Matters, 2021), so anti-oppressive practices mean considering your practices towards every individual and groups. Dr Daniel has identified within her work that each child and family bring their own identity, values and their unique funds of knowledge.

We live in a country where most of the population has been co-existing with diverse cultural and racial ethnicity since the Second World War, when there was a need for immigration to support skilled jobs. It fundamentally changed the ecology of Britain's population. No matter how well-meaning we are as a human being, we are also able to subject others to bias. We are all influenced by the society that we live in.

Explained in her discussions, in the wake of the COVID- 19 pandemic and the other factors affecting our society in the Early Years, it was a turning point for many to wake up and think about the impact that these were having on our children within the Early Childhood sector. Mainly depicting the focus of Dr Daniel's work in the Early Years, she has explored all aspects of society today and why it is so important for Early Childhood professionals to engage in these dialogues of discussion, which inform our practices. So, let's look at these in greater detail:

Taking the Equality Act 2010, which is the baseline of Dr Daniel's discussion, and then applying this to current affairs was a good starting point for us within the sector. Before now we had seen many events as secular, but focusing on oppression it became clear that voices that were oppressed, the children in our settings who have not been given an adequate opportunity to thrive, collectively started to matter. It is quite sad when you come to think of it, and it is nothing new. The Equality Act 2010 is now 12 years old, so it's no wonder that the oppressed voices are now turning to us all and saying, what are you going to do about it. Collectively, we can do something.

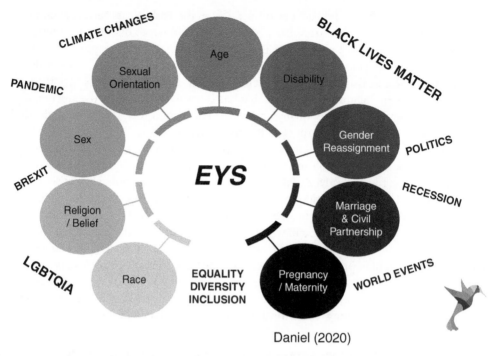

Daniel (2020)

Figure 9.2   Current trends in the early years – Early Years Reviews (2020)

Figure 9.2 shows the current turmoil that our society is in. Dr Daniel explores her concept further by explaining that the current trends within our society are in fact in turmoil. The question for us as professionals on the ground is how can we do something about this? Well, Dr Daniel explores that we have the power to be able to do something about all of this. Early Years and the education, the learning, the opportunities and the environment you give to children can make a huge impact on a child's life chance.

WHERE DOES EQUALITY, DIVERSITY AND INCLUSION BEGIN?

Equality, diversity and inclusion requires more than just treating everyone the same. There is a great difference between equity and equality. Equality is about fairness through treating everyone the same regardless of need; however, equity achieves this by treating people differently depending on their need. As a professional it is vital that all children and families are included and celebrated, but at the same time it is important that Early Childhood practitioners are aware of the significant emotional, physical and social barriers that children may encounter in accessing services such as education, health and development and social aspects of a child's life. Values are not universal and therefore as professionals we may need to change some of our thinking. Children and their families may require extra support to develop trust so that they can be valued as individuals within your setting. Thinking about this, how do you overcome some of these value barriers within your practice? Let's look at some below.

REFLECTIVE PRACTICE EXERCISE

In your setting do you ever say the following?
We wear coats when we go outside, even if it's cold or raining.
Boys and Girls play together.
It's great to get messy
We eat with our knives and forks.

REFLECTIVE QUESTIONS

When was the last time you said any of the above?
How are you consciously trying to overcome the thinking of your own values?
Have you explored your own children's and family values within the setting?

CREATING SAFE SPACES

Dr Daniel explores in her discussions and research how we can create safe spaces to develop a culture of openness and critique. Safe spaces in the Early Years have become a new concept, one which was highlighted by Dr Daniel in the *LGBTQIA Early Years Magazine* (2021). In an article titled 'Reframing Safe Spaces', she explores how this concept can be applied to anti oppressive practices and systemic oppression within the Early Years. For many, this was a concept which the sector hadn't heard of before. Publishing materials on how to reframe this was a positive move by Dr Valerie Daniel. So much so we started to see open discussions on social media, articles were citing the work of Daniel (2021) and we were now exploring new concepts of how to tackle oppressive practices within the Early Years.

Daniel explores the concepts of creating safe spaces and discusses that the information out there regarding them is rife with disinformation (*LGBTQIA Early Years Magazine*, 2021), which in turn creates a sense of confusion and misunderstanding about important social and political issues within Early Childhood, such as racism, political changes and anti-oppressive practices. Daniel goes on to explore that this in turn curtails any progress we can make with regards to systemic oppression. The concept of a safe space is a protected time and place for open debate without reprisals. Outside of that context if a professional displays any unacceptable behaviour which in turn can become a pattern of behaviour, this will need to go through the necessary disciplinary procedures.

A 'safe space' is not a physical location. It is a concept which you develop as an ethos within your setting. Daniel 'explores that it is a commitment to providing a supportive and respectful learning and working environment' (*LGBTQIA Early Years Magazine*, 2021, p. 16).

BEING A LEADER - CREATING A SAFE SPACE

We generally work in environments where people feel afraid to speak up openly about their feelings or discuss aspects of unfair practices.

Yee stated that 'how we see the world shapes who we choose to be – and sharing compelling experiences can frame the way we treat each other, for the better' (2019). When you are a leader of a team within an Early Childhood setting, it is important to be aware that solid leadership, being a good communicator and having access to continual professional development is what essentially drives it. Understanding each other and each other's values plays a huge part in how you create a safe space. We live and work within diverse communities, so despite ideas of absolutism (the political doctrine and practice of unlimited centralised authority and absolute sovereignty, as vested especially in a monarch or dictator), we are faced every day with a range of human variances – race, gender, sexual orientation, physical abilities, age, social class, sex, religion, political beliefs, as well as personal backgrounds and ethical value systems.

Being a leader comes with its own barriers to being able to create a safe space. Some leaders may also be an employer, and it is important that they feel included and that their values are heard and understood. Leaders need to be in tune with the fact that the environment plays a big part in creating a safe space for professionals and the children. There is a need for leaders and managers to be up to date with contemporary discussions and being prepared for safe spaces within their settings. 'Leaders are objectively aware, early education work environments are children's learning; children depend on their educators who are not only skills, but have their well-being and needs supported, too. Just as children's environments can support or impeded their learning, teachers work environments can promote or hinder practice and ongoing skills development' (Schlieber and McLean, 2020).

REFLECTIVE PRACTICE EXERCISE

EXPLORING RACIAL DIFFERENCES THROUGH SAFE SPACES

There are several myths associated with racial difference and these myths have seeped into the fabric of our society. You could argue that these have also seeped into our own subconscious, by making us think in many ways including how we interact with children of a different race to us. You could argue that the stereotyping of Black people, for example, in society today is deeply embedded into the culture.

There is a need to understand within the Early Childhood sector that political and legislative decisions are still entwined with white males and these negative biases often find their way into our own practices through policy formation. There is a constant trend today to continually discriminate against Black people and we must break this down through our own consciousness. If we reflect on this example against other forms of oppression within our society, we then begin to understand why a safe space for open debate is essential to be able to make the changes we desire for our children and families.

(Continued)

(Continued)

PUTTING IT INTO PRACTICE

There are many ways you can create a safe space – let's look at how you can make a start by introducing some of these activities:

1. Anonymous Surveys – Looking at the reasons why, you can look at the survey knowing what people feel rather than who feels that way. The survey can be collated through utilising a raw data collection, comments, and then analysed against your settings ethos and philosophy as a setting.
2. The String Conversation – This exercise is making sure that everyone has an opportunity to speak and share any ideas. They do not have to speak if they don't want to, and they can throw the string to someone else. This activity will help to manage the louder and more confident voices and allows the quieter ones a chance to be heard.
3. Fishbowl Exercise – This is a forum where you can bring difficult situations and unpick them through direct challenge. This exercise needs to be completed with a team which has matured through concerted efforts to be able to build up relationships and withstand any direct approaches within the activity.
4. Round Table Exercise – Bringing together areas which are associated with equalities. This is a forum where discussions on changes happen. This can be both personal and professional, what is affecting us as professionals. So, discussions around race, gender, sexual identity, to name a few are discussed. Daniel (2021, p. 17) https://lgbtqearlyyears.org/product/lgbtqia-early-years-magazine-downloadable-copy/.

A safe space is not always a feel-good, happy space where you should be shying away from uncomfortable conversations. It is a space in which Early Years settings can deal with differences head on and by doing this, learn from one another and create meaningful relationships. Being able to develop our true authentic self is a common approach with the Early Years. It is important that we practice what we preach within this context. Safe Spaces should be a place where you can collectively devise protocols together for our differences, as well as safe space activities, with the main elements being:

- No one should feel upset, ashamed or angry.
- If there are any nagging feelings, then these need to be raised.
- Sometimes you must agree to disagree, this is okay.
- Having a clear course of action and next steps.

Remember it is not about being right, but it is about winning hearts and minds to make a difference for the future of the children in our care.

EQUALITY, DIVERSITY AND INCLUSION IN PRACTICE

This chapter has given enough dialogue around the implications of oppressive implications on the child, but let's not forget that equality, diversity and inclusion is not a linear concept. It sits within the context of the child. Daniel explores all these ideas by keeping the child at the centre of Early Years pedagogy by exploring the need for anti-racist practices. Therefore, it is a whole philosophical approach to practice within your setting. The discussions, the research which is highlighted in the context of leadership and management, allow you to think about the context of your own position within Early Childhood and being able to focus on what we do and the impact we have on each child.

We have an opportunity to trailblaze an inclusive dialogue through Early Years practices by allowing conversations to be at the centre of your own practice and begin to change the way we think, reflecting on our own value bases. This can be done in many ways, and one way it can be achieved is through approaches such as following a curriculum. The Non-Statutory Guidance for the Early Years Birth to Five Matters (2021) has been able to do this effectively. It has started to tackle anti-oppressive practice by discussing inequalities directly within our society, mirrored with the work that Dr Daniel is doing, calling it out and highlighting anti-oppressive practice, including LGBTQ, sexual orientation and racism. At the heart of all the discussion should be the child and what they bring in terms of their uniqueness.

What do we mean by 'the unique child' and why is it such a well-used term? Well, it is what it says on the tin 'The Unique Child', most of us have heard it, but do we truly embody it? My definition of the Unique Child is:

> Every child is a unique child, one which learns continuously and can be resilient, capable, confident and self-assured.

(Bradbury, 2021a)

Early educators need to fundamentally know what it means for our practices to be taken forward, but also the fact that it relies heavily on us knowing what being child-centred means and fundamentally supporting the child as a unique and individual person. Children continuously mature in all aspects of development, at their own pace, and all of them do this in their own individual ways. The inclusion of the Unique Child means that the child and the community that they come from is valued, which means that they are not discriminated against. By supporting the Unique Child, you can support the child's resilience which then supports their well-being and child which is able to flourish and reach their full potential. The holistic child development abilities of a child's uniqueness is an integral part of children's emotional, social, environmental and spiritual health.

CASE STUDY

Exploring Buildings

Jennifer has been working at Tiny tot's preschool since she qualified in the 1990s. A leader within the setting and is the lead for curriculum, staff planning and resources. In Jennifer's room is Rammy, a preschool assistant, and Karim, an Early Years Teacher practitioner. The team meet regularly to

(Continued)

discuss themes and plan for the week ahead. Next week's topic of activities are buildings, and the focus is where we live.

Do you do activities like this? If so, what do you do for this topic?

Ask yourself the following questions:

- *Have you ever been around the local area?*
- *Do you know the home conditions that the children come from?*
- *Have you taken the child's individual circumstances in to play here?*
- *What resources are you using? If it's a book, does the book have all the buildings you need to be represented?*
- *Can the activities represent their own depiction of their buildings? Explore buildings further afield, for example, places of worship, shops, etc.*

INCLUSIVE NURTURING CARE – LINKING TO BAVOLEK AND BRONFENBRENNER

Inclusive Nurturing Care is a concept in which we all strive to achieve within our role as Early Childhood practitioners. Just like in Chapter 1 where we explored Dr Bavolek's ideas about the role of nurturing and how this supports the emotional well-being of the child, you could argue that so does making sure that each child is nurtured to the point of feeling a sense of belonging.

Dr Daniel's work around child-centred practices and nurturing individual needs could be linked to the theory of Bronfenbrenner (see Chapter 2 – Bronfenbrenner).

Bronfenbrenner research highlighted the continual oppression of society and experiences which impinged on the child and parents' lives and society more widely such as:

- Poverty
- Racism
- Sexism
- And more recently, within the context of his theory emphasising the growing trend of homophobia against the ever-changing family structures we now have in the 21st century.

Further to this, his research identified the importance of the different 'levels' of the child's place in society and how they interacted with all aspects of this. Even though there are many criticisms of Bronfenbrenner's theory on how his findings link to the practical work within our settings, it has given a new open door towards the study of the connections of child development and has supported past government programmes for children and families, such as Sure Start Children's Centres developed by the Labour Government in 1999.

There is a link between Bronfenbrenner theory and that of Daniel (2019) which can support children through their individual and unique experiences. The chaotic approach to current cuts on policies in Early Childhood, families and children's provision has proven to be a real opportunity to reflect on these changes and the impact that they are having on our practice for children in our care. This has been researched heavily by Daniel (2019) with the focus being Early Years and the transition of policy across a 20-year period to date. There has been a continual priority about UK policy reforms and the continual reframing of the Early Years regulatory frameworks. The most important factor that Daniel explores is that of the current operation of the Early Years, where she calls it a 'kaleidoscope' with regards to many policy drivers including qualifications, experiences, professional heritages and the continual debate about what is best for children (Daniel, 2019). This links to Bronfenbrenner's five critical processes which we will now explore further.

FIVE CRITICAL PROCESSES

Bronfenbrenner continued his work in Early Childhood, proposing five critical processes for positive human development:

1. Patterns of shared interactions are regular, over an extended period, so that the child develops a strong, mutual emotional attachment with one or more persons (a parent, carer, sibling or grandparent, for example) who care unconditionally about the child's well-being.
2. These shared interactions promote the child's responsiveness to other aspects of the immediate environment
3. Another person to encourage and support the intimate care, demonstrating love and affection for the child.
4. Family members and nursery staff, linking to the unique child, the history and the position that the child and family have come from.
5. Public policies and practices are needed that ensure stability, time, status and respect for whole communities supporting the first 1001 days of a child's life.

(Bradbury, 2021)

Ultimately we need to be open about the true oppressive factors that can impinge on a child's development. More recently, the scope around developing a loving pedagogy by Grimmer (2020) and more pertinent being able to ask ourselves questions about what are we doing here in the role I am in? (Figure 9.3).

Tips to incorporate Daniel's principles in your early years practice

1. Make sure that you are familiar with the concept of child development and start to link these to your everyday practices.
2. Familiarise yourself with concepts today, such as Developing a Loving Pedagogy, The Unique Child, The Voice of the Child, Anti-Racism, Anti-oppressive practices, legislation, and policy and then think about how theory such as Bronfenbrenner and Grimmer has supported these approaches with your children and families.
3. Value your expertise and judgements, but also value the focus on which the practice you offer has been developed through research, discussion and continual reflection.
4. You know your children and develop an ethos within your setting that promotes every child being successful in life and becoming resilient and emotionally intelligent human beings.

Figure 9.3 Tips to incorporate Daniel's principles within your Early Years practice

CONCLUSION

To support the development of the unique child, and the physical environment we provide for children in our settings is an important factor to take forwards. For a child to be able to develop a holistic approach to love, equality, diversity, and inclusion and nurturing so we can start with child development first and foremost and then move to questioning ourselves with our values. Who truly decides on what is right and wrong when it comes to our children, and what should be taught to our children? Moreover, being able to question the power balance which we have in our settings and what we do with them. That alone can cause many issues when it comes to stifling children's development, and we see this continually when we make those decisions surrounding what we should and shouldn't teach children when it comes to anti-oppressive practices. It's all or nothing. It needs to start with the child being loved, becoming empowered and then within that environment they are ready to learn. We hold the key to be able to do this.

FURTHER READING

Bradbury, A. (2021) How to nurture children and enhance your environment in the Early Years. *Kinderly.* https://kinderly.co.uk/2020/12/17/how-to-nurture-children-and-enhance-your-early-years-environment/

Bradbury, A. and Pemberton, L. (2020) The early years inclusion revolution. *Famly.* https://www.famly.co/blog/early-years-inclusion-revolution

Grimmer, T. (2021) *Developing a Loving Pedagogy in the Early Years: How Love Fits with Professional Practice.* London: David Fulton Book.

Macblain, S. (2021) *Children's Learning in Early Childhood: Learning Theories in Practice 0–7.*

10

MARGARET MCMILLAN AND GRACE OWEN

NURSERY WARS: DEBATING AND DEFINING THE MODERN NURSERY

By Pam Jarvis

KEY DEFINITIONS

Nursery schools	In today's world, we divide Early Years education and care into defined categories, such as day care, nursery class, nursery school, PVI playgroups, etc. In the early days of the NSA, all settings were labelled 'nursery schools'. Do you think this blurring of agendas exacerbated the arguments between McMillan and Owen?
Froebelian practices	While McMillan was a strong critic of the nursery classes supported by the Froebelians on the NSA, she was for many years actively involved in the Frobelian Society and wrote articles for their journals.[1] What do you understand as 'Froebelian practices'?
Play-based learning	We talk today of 'play-based learning', a concept enthusiastically espoused by both McMillan and Owen. What differences would you identify in their emphases within this broad definition?
Curriculum	The concept of a 'curriculum' for Early Years would have been quite alien to both McMillan and Owen, while in contemporary England in particular, it tends to be accepted as a conventional underpinning to Early Years practice. Do you think this has been a largely positive, negative or mixed development and why?

INTRODUCTION: THE EVOLUTION OF THE MODERN BRITISH NURSERY

Modern Early Years education and care evolved in Britain across the latter half of the 19th century, as the effects of the Industrial Revolution became evident. The deprived conditions in which the urban poor existed fuelled a growing public concern about the poor health of inner-city children.[2] This became even more obvious following the instigation of compulsory state education for 5–10 year olds in 1870.[3]

The Charity Organisation Society (COS) was founded in London in 1869[4] triggering the emergence of middle-class female charity workers tasked to instil 'good habits' into working class mothers: 'the benevolent and astute judgement of middle class women… was imagined to bring about the transformation of the character of the poor'.[5] As these previously sheltered and often unworldly women ventured into homes in the most deprived areas of industrial cities, it was somewhat inevitable, however genuine their intentions, that they would 'frequently misread the survival strategies of the urban poor, in their belief that bourgeois domestic arrangements were the only current standard of home management'.[6] It was not long before many felt the impetus to extend their mission by drawing the preschool children of deprived families into a more 'enlightened' care and education regime that they (with the financial support of their donors) would seek to provide.

Those who created such regimes did not always agree on how they should be organised, however. The heated exchanges between Margaret McMillan (1860–1931) and Grace Owen (1873–1965), respectively the first president and first secretary of Nursery School Association (NSA) are an ideal example of this debate. Their documentation by their student, Abigail Adams Eliot (1892–1992) shines a fascinating light on how the organisation of the modern Early Years education and care was passionately debated and constructed.

THE CHRISTIAN SOCIALIST MISSIONARY: MARGARET MCMILLAN

The McMillan sisters were born in Westchester County New York, Rachel in 1859 and Margaret in 1860; however, following the death of the sisters' father and youngest sister in 1865, their mother took them back to her family home in Inverness. By 1888, the sisters had become enthusiastic converts to Christian Socialism.[7] In 1889, they moved to London to begin their mission. Margaret began to build a reputation as a skilled orator, delivering speeches on the benefits of socialism at Hyde Park Corner.[8] She was consequently offered a salaried position by the Independent Labour Party (ILP) in Bradford[9] delivering a programme of Socialist lectures to audiences across Yorkshire and Lancashire. She was elected to the Bradford School Board as a representative of the ILP in November 1894[10] and quickly realised that the conditions in under which children were required to attend school significantly added to their misery.

Many of the children worked half days in local mills, and most were poorly nourished, frequently infested with lice and ringworm, and in generally poor health. Much of this was caused by the extreme poverty of their families and a lack of even basic amenities, which meant that maintaining personal hygiene was fraught with difficulty. It was common for mothers to sew children into their clothes at the beginning of winter,[11] hoping that this would protect against colds and chills, meaning that neither the child nor the clothes were properly washed for many months.

Margaret McMillan took it upon herself to create an innovative health promotion programme operating within schools in the city. Consequently, Bradford became the first education authority in the country to provide baths and showers on school premises from 1897[12] and free school meals in 1902.[13] However, in 1902 a new education bill abolished the school boards, giving control and management of elementary schools to the District and County Councils to which women could not be elected.[14] Margaret, struggling with her bitter disappointment at the inability to continue with her programme,[15] decided to relocate to London,[16] moving in with Rachel who was working as a travelling teacher of health and hygiene.

The sisters continued to campaign for child health, and in 1907 their efforts led to the passing of a parliamentary bill stipulating the compulsory medical inspection of school children.[17] On the strength of this success, they managed to obtain a £5000 bursary to open a school clinic in a Deptford, South East London, which proved to be a great success.[18] But it quickly became something of a revolving door:

> Nurse Spiker at the clinic said 'it's all a waste of time. These children come here, are cured and go but in two weeks, sometimes less they are back again. All these ailments could be prevented, their cause is dirt, lack of light and sun, fresh air and good food'.[19]

The McMillans consequently experimented with further projects that would allow them to provide a nurturing environment for local children that would proactively protect their health. The first venture was an overnight 'camp' in the garden of the house in which the clinic was located, where camp beds, washing facilities and a nutritious breakfast were provided for local children.[20]

A small 'camp school' for children aged 5–14 followed in 1912.[21] However, this soon ran into funding problems, and Margaret's attention turned towards providing a 'baby camp' for infants under five. She decreed: 'we must open our doors to the toddlers, Rachel... we must plan the right kind of environment for them and give them sunshine, fresh air and good food *before* they become rickety and diseased'.[22]

The sisters acquired suitable premises,[23] and the initiative which became locally known as 'the nursery' opened in 1914. They focused upon the provision of cleanliness, sunshine, fresh air, good food and plenty of time to play in the garden. Sadly, Rachel died during early 1917,[24] but as World War I drew to a close in 1918, the renamed 'Rachel McMillan Open Air Nursery School'[25] was proclaimed as a huge success, gaining local, national and international fame for its successes, with respect not only to vastly improved health in the children of the district but also to the superior intellectual and social development demonstrated in the children's behaviour and achievements. It was visited by a steady stream of dignitaries including Queen Mary, Rudolph Steiner, George Bernard Shaw, many MPs and the Prime Minister Stanley Baldwin who wrote to McMillan: 'I shall never forget my visit to you and to your children; it was a revelation.'[26]

During the 1920s a range of national benefits that could be addressed through national public health initiatives were beginning to seem an achievable reality.[27] The Education Act 1921 made provision for grants to organise nursery schools for children over two years old and under five years old to be disseminated and overseen by Local Education Authorities.[28] The establishment of the NSA followed in 1923, with Margaret McMillan as its first president.[29]

THE PIONEERING PEDAGOGUE: GRACE OWEN

Grace Owen (1873–1965) was elected as the first Honorary Secretary to the NSA,[30] becoming McMillan's closest colleague in one of the most ambitious Early Years care and education enterprises of all time: to shape the framework of a standard nursery school within Great Britain as a whole. At this time, Owen was already 'a pivotal figure at the City of Manchester training school for nursery schoolteachers',[31] the concept of the nursery school being already 30 years old in Manchester when the McMillans set up their 'baby camp'.

Sir William Mather established a free Kindergarten in Salford in 1873, basing the practice in the nursery upon those of Friedrich Froebel (1785–1852), the originator of the term 'kindergarten' for the Play and Activity Institute he founded in 1837 at Bad Blankenburg in Germany. Mather founded the Manchester Kindergarten Association in 1873[32] and was a significant figure in the establishment of the English Froebel Society London in 1874, which continues to the present day as the National Froebel Foundation.[33] Froebellian pedagogy emphasised a child-centred approach and active learning with particular emphasis on outdoor play,[34] in many ways quite similar to the regime the McMillan sisters had cobbled together.

Grace Owen was a veteran of a long training process that emphasised pedagogy over the political and religious social justice impetus that had inspired the McMillan sisters. Owen was a half generation younger than the McMillans, trained in Froebelian methods at the Blackheath Kindergarten Training College. She had then gone on to achieve a degree in education at the University of Columbia in the United States, graduating in 1905. On her return to England, she joined the staff of the University of Manchester, lecturing in education.[35]

During the early decades of the 20th century, it was unusual for women to be graduates of a university at all, let alone to be given the chance to acquire the international sophistication that Owen brought to her practice. She became principal of the Manchester Kindergarten Training College, recognised in 1917 by the Board of Education as an endorsed supplier of teacher training, several years prior to the Rachel McMillan Nursery's recognition as a training centre. Owen became the Organising Secretary of the Manchester and Salford Council for Day Nurseries and Nursery Schools,[36] and in 1920, she created a 'demonstration nursery school' at 61 Shakespeare Street, Manchester.[37]

To paint a picture of the meeting between these two women for a modern audience, it may be helpful to envision McMillan in the role of a media star, who could provide the new association with punchy publicity via her passionate and politicised speeches, which could always be relied upon to 'wow' an audience. Owen, by contrast, was the consummate professional who had steadfastly carved out a path for herself in a world where it was very rare for women to rise to the academic and professional level that she had attained.

In this sense then, McMillan was the 'heart' of the NSA, well equipped to blaze a trail for social justice, while Owen was the 'head', who could use her depth of pedagogical knowledge and experience to create a profession that would take its place beside school teaching in an era becoming increasingly receptive to the concept of a public responsibility for the health and education of children.[38]

It was certainly a promising plan. But it didn't work out as expected.

THE VOICE OF THE NEXT GENERATION: ABIGAIL ADAMS ELIOT

In June 1921, Radcliffe College graduate Abigail Eliot, the 29-year-old daughter of a wealthy American family landed in England to spend six months at the McMillan nursery studying its practice, with the intention of setting up a similar nursery in Boston. Eliot had five years' experience of social work in the Boston area, followed by a year studying at Oxford University in England from 1919 to 1920. She was funded by the Boston Women's Education Association and supervised by Mrs Henry Greenleaf Pearson, the wife of a wealthy Massachusetts Institute of Technology lecturer and author.[39]

When Eliot returned to Boston, she achieved her ambition to create and lead a successful nursery school, concluding her working life as the director of the Eliot-Pearson Department of Child Study at Tufts University in Medford, Massachusetts.[40] But before her independent professional practice began, however, the situation in which she was placed gave her the opportunity to document the differences between McMillan and Owen for posterity, in the letters that she sent back to Boston.

Initially, Eliot described her disappointment with the environment in which she was placed:

8th June 1921: I am established in one of the hostels of the school in a tiny room of the third floor of a building overlooking the school, which is a large garden here in the midst of a most sordid district.[41]

It was soon evident that she had some practice differences with Margaret McMillan, in particular that the practice in the nursery was not classically Froebelian:

14th June 1921: Under Miss McMillan there is a Principal or Headmistress of the school, Miss Stevinson. It seems that her educational ideas don't agree in toto with Miss McMillan. She is Froebel trained and leans in that direction.[42]

After a month had elapsed, she wrote more frankly to Mrs Pearson about some significant concerns, particularly her experience of Margaret McMillan as an extremely difficult supervisor:

20th July 1921: There are things here that make me angry and things that make me sad... Miss McMillan is so jealous of Mme Montessori's work that none of the Montessori apparatus can be used here...Miss McMillan is... so sure her ways are the only right ways that she will not even discuss such questions with people... it almost seems as if she lacks the scientific spirit.[43]

Eliot had some time off in August and immediately rekindled connections with friends she had made at Oxford, in order to find some respite in an environment she found more to her taste.

3rd August 1921: This week I am giving myself the luxury of living in...Bloomsbury. I couldn't stand Deptford any longer... I am glad of a week in comfortable quarters with good food... and a comfortable bed... fresh air and use of a nice bathroom and pleasant people to talk to.[44]

A fortnight later, she wrote to her mother from Bradford, where she was visiting some of the schools operating along the same practice lines as the McMillan nursery:

16th August 1921: The longer I am here, the more I discover that we [referring to those who embrace McMillan practices in general] scarcely speak the same language.... [Bradford] is supposed to be the most admired in education. Yet all I can think to describe it is sordid, dark, dingy and ugly.[45]

Less than a fortnight later, however, she sent another, more cheerful letter, having made the acquaintance of someone she found much more in tune with her own ideas about Early Years education:

25th August 1921: I had the pleasure of going to a tiny village on the edge of the North York Moors... to see Miss Grace Owen.[46]

She elaborated on her greater regard for Owen to Mrs Pearson:

21st August 1921: [Owen] told me so many things of most intense value that I... wish I had a Dictaphone with me... it seems as if she was heaven sent to put me on the right track... the greatest joy of all is her scientific spirit.[47]

When Eliot returned to London, she tried to tell McMillan about her discussions with Owen, which clearly did not go well. McMillan had previously expressed extreme displeasure when she learned that Eliot had arranged a visit to a nursery class in a Manchester elementary school 'on the ground I would learn nothing from it. Because of Miss McMillan's disapproval I took only one working day off, but I went... it was an important part of my English education in regard to nursery schools.'[48]

She reported McMillan's comments to Mrs Pearson:

26th August 1921: I am sick at heart today and must blow it out on someone. You seem to be the logical person to whom to do so... Miss McMillan was... scornful. She says she cannot get along with Miss Owen [and] doesn't like her... [McMillan] is an old woman and a pig-headed one.[49]

A week later, Eliot formally requested a transfer to Owen's school. Mrs Pearson's reply is unfortunately not in the record, but it seems the request was not granted, as Eliot remained at the Deptford Nursery for the remainder of her placement.[50] In 1960, she wrote vividly on her memories of Margaret McMillan as a professional mentor: 'Such sincerity, self-confidence and commitment... "treat each child as if he were your own"... a commanding manner and voice, she could frighten and dismay a young student.'[51]

While Eliot's accounts cannot be considered wholly objective, they are useful in shedding some light on the differences that created the heated debates that arose between McMillan and Owen when they were tasked to work closely together on the NSA. Eliot provides a clear account of the contrast between Owen's academic and professional ethos and McMillan's emotional, spiritually driven conviction, from which disagreements were destined to arise.

THE NURSERY SCHOOL ASSOCIATION: BORN INTO CONTROVERSY

Candidate suitability for nursery teacher training became an immediate bone of contention between McMillan and Owen. In Britain, the Froebellian tradition in which Owen had been schooled gave rise to a teacher training process which prepared students to teach three to six-year-olds via indoor, free-flow play-based learning with an adjacent outdoor area, similar to current conventions. Provision was frequently located in 'Nursery Classes' in primary schools led by a trained nursery teacher, children were allocated to classes of approximately 30–35, and attended for a similarly structured school day to that offered to older children.

McMillan's practice had, by contrast, grown up around outdoor provision for disadvantaged children, where they spent most of the day playing in the open air, and in the shelters attached to the front of the buildings. The cohorts were much bigger than those in the typical nursery class, but staff were far more numerous; however a significant percentage of these were unqualified 'helpers.' Pupils attended for significantly longer hours, typically between 8 a.m. and 5.30 p.m., and the McMillan Nursery routinely admitted children who were not yet three.

McMillan insisted that children should spend most of their waking day at nursery and that the nursery should be responsible for providing all their main meals, plus the necessary social and emotional foundation for robust mental health. In 1925, she emphatically defended these principles, proposing that 'the nursery *class* [was] an extravagant investment failing to provide a good return',[52] insisting that the children in her nursery required more 'nurture' than they would get from attending a nursery class. She wrote privately to fellow Christian socialist Robert Blatchford in 1929:

> Now I am battling for a nine-hour day for nursery school children. We open at a quarter to eight. We close at five thirty. It is not much use to little ones to rattle them in and out of school as they do. <u>They need nurture.</u>[53]... we must have a new conception of <u>school</u> that it should be a nurture centre as well as a place for lessons...[54]

When it came to the type and number of practitioners required, McMillan had a very different view to Grace Owen. She commented:

> After sad experience we gave up nurses and turned to teachers. Then came new revelations... those who came first were shocked; they had never seen the inside of a slum home....[55]

McMillan insisted her students live in a building close by the nursery so they got 'to know their new neighbours. They have to get some idea of housing, of the cost of food, and the needs of a family who live always on the brink of a financial precipice!'[56] This, of course was the practice that had so horrified Abigail Eliot, vividly outlined in her letters.

In a NSA meeting held on 3rd January 1925, H. Ward, a member of the Board of Education, clearly outlined a point of view in line with that of Owen:

> We must be very careful to have teachers properly trained for this important period of school life. A girl with a secondary education and a motherly heart is not enough. At this age we have the great habit-forming period, and the younger the child is, the more rapid is his intellectual growth. This, then requires the skill of the wisest and best teachers we have.[57]

McMillan spoke in response to this statement and was summarised in the minutes as having said that

> ...All the members [of the NSA] had the same object in view – the ideal education of the child under five. In her opinion, however, the nursery class was in danger, vitiating the real aim and refusing the very people, who with widely differing qualifications, might as

students help in the work. The nursery *school* needed an attendant to every six children, and it needed to have large numbers of children, with students of every type under trained teachers to provide the right care and adequate culture at a reasonable cost. She considered the nursery *class* an extravagant investment failing to provide a good return.[58]

However, she was not successful in making any impression upon Grace Owen. As the secretary of the NSA, Owen was responsible for its communications, and in 1925 its statement of policy clearly stipulated one trained teacher to 35 children.[59] McMillan struck back in a bulletin from the NSA circulated in 1927, reiterating the pattern of practice and staffing in her nursery, referring to 'new method of staffing and building.' She explained that 150 children could be supervised by only 'one trained teacher per shelter' as long as there were plenty of untrained helpers.[60]

An NSA Bulletin produced in 1936 contains a 1930 quote from Grace Owen proposing that 'the nursery class should.... function as a small nursery.' An additional note in her handwriting clearly reiterates the formula of 1 teacher plus two helpers to 35 children which was present in the NSA policy document of 1925.[61]

Correspondence between Manchester-based Shena D. Simon and Grace Owen in early 1929 indicates the depth of the disagreement between Owen and McMillan. Simon comments that she is 'very interested' in the NSA but wants to know whether 'it will be made quite clear that "nursery school" includes "nursery class",' continuing:

Some people associated with the nursery school movement are definitely hostile to them [nursery classes]... I should not like to be helping an operation that would be in any way hostile to properly constituted nursery classes.[62]

Owen replied to the following day:

I think I understand your question perfectly... the president of our association is openly hostile to nursery classes... the NSA is however as stated in its constitution... pledged to work for the effective working of nursery school classes in the Education Act of 1918... I heartily endorsed the nursery school policy of the Manchester Education Committee of a few years ago... [which was] nursery school departments in new schools.[63]

The dichotomy between Owen's concept of a nursery *education* and McMillan's concept of *nurture* within an early years environment thus clearly emerges from these historical debates. McMillan's emphasis was upon social and emotional nurture, which could be supplied by untrained workers, providing that they were sufficiently 'motherly', under the direction of a highly trained teacher. However, for Owen, the pedagogy delivered by trained teaching staff was the nursery's central purpose. This fundamental disagreement went on to become a significant sticking point, obstructing the construction of a cohesive NSA policy for practice.

While there are inevitably gaps in the record relating to this growing schism, it is clear that on 16th April 1929, McMillan formally wrote to Owen, communicating her intention to resign from the presidency of the NSA.[64] On 7th May, the NSA responded, asking for further information on the reasons relating to this decision.[65] There is no concrete evidence to indicate this was ever provided. On 18th May McMillan submitted her letter of resignation.[66] She wrote to fellow founder NSA member Lillian de Lissa on 8th May warning of her resignation intentions, whilst reassuring de Lissa of her admiration for Owen, stating that there must be no bad feeling within the NSA.[67] On 18th May, the same day as her resignation, McMillan wrote to de Lissa again, informing her that it had been 'quite a trial resigning from the presidentship [sic]'.[68] On 20th June, the NSA discussed McMillan's resignation and agreed to temporarily replace her with de Lissa,[69] and on 21st June, McMillan wrote to Owen that the NSA episode had left her with 'a sense of failure and regret'.[70]

McMillan's position was further discussed in the notes of the NSA on 20th June:

> ...Miss McMillan stated that her resignation was 'the result of a growing recognition that I am not in your movement. The salvation of the children of the poorest class will not come through the school that is advocated by the NSA'... [she proposed that] the statement of the principles of the NSA [published in 1925] was never properly discussed by the members.[71]

...thus implying that Owen had acted without consultation, an accusation not supported by the other officials on the Committee.[72]

In March 1930, McMillan wrote to Grace Owen to decline an invitation to write a chapter on outdoor nursery accommodation in a book that Owen was editing on the behalf of the NSA:

> I would do anything to help the open air nursery school movement, but in obscuring my sister's and my own [sic] you are really hindering it.... If I wrote in your book I should be perhaps in conflict with other writers... I will not be in conflict at all.... I have learned my lesson and will not ally myself again.[73]

McMillan died a year later, in March 1931. Her posthumous fame swiftly began to eclipse that of the other founder members of the NSA; Jane Read comments that McMillan was 'designated a "prophetess" by LCC Inspectors Philip Ballard, Gwendolen Sanson and Miss E. Stevinson' in evidence to the Hadow Committee of 1933.[74] However, Owen's 'nursery class' strategy endured, dominating the culture of British early years education to the present day.[75]

It is quite possible that McMillan was too hasty to take offence and remove herself from the NSA. The woman that Eliot so vividly describes in her letters depicts a peppery character, with a tendency to take extreme and dramatic positions, particularly when she felt she had been 'crossed'. Approached differently, might Owen have been prepared to negotiate? Within the 1936 bulletin in which she reiterates her formula for nursery organisation, she additionally makes the point that the organisation of nurseries must recognise 'the type of accommodation provided [and]... must necessarily vary with the local circumstances'.[76] Perhaps if McMillan had been more inclined to compromise, a more complex concept of Early Years care and education practices that could draw on different practices in different situations a more flexible vision of Early Years education and care would have been bequeathed to later generations.

HISTORICAL THEORY INTO MODERN PRACTICE: MCMILLAN AND OWEN UNITED?

The national importance of state-funded nursery education rose during the Second World War years of 1939–1945, and declined over the following five decades before moving back onto the New Labour government agenda in the National Childcare Strategy of 1998 'in the context of workfarism [and]... lucrative childcare markets'.[77]

This raised the ghosts of Owen and McMillan with respect to a potential clash of agendas, but one that was framed in the context of a very different society; the ravages of family poverty endured in Britain, most prevalently within inner city areas, as had been the case in McMillan's time. But there was also a growing demand for a 'school readiness' curriculum in from aspirational middle-class families who had grown up within an established Welfare State. The initial iteration of the Early Years Foundation Stage (2007)[78] was intended to address both agendas, with the Children's Centre initiative intended to coordinate support for families in need; and in the short period that they were able to operate, Prime Minister Gordon Brown commended them for making a 'real and genuine difference'[79] children and their families.

In 2010, a Conservative-led Coalition Government closed the vast majority of children's centres[80] citing an austerity agenda in response to the world financial crisis of 2007–2008.[81] In 2020, a Conservative Government commissioned a major review of the Early Years Foundation Stage. The resulting iteration drew accusations from the Early Years sector that it was 'too narrow and too formal for young children',[82] a debate which continues at time of publication.

So, how might Owen and McMillan respond to this situation? Perhaps they may have found themselves more united than they had been in their own time, joining forces to preserve the play-based learning that both passionately espoused. While it is clear that they viewed the terrain of nursery education from somewhat different positions, the current relentless top-down focus on children's 'readiness' for each successive stage of education and 'performance' in frequent narrowly framed assessment tasks would be alien to both. Again, there may have been differences in emphases. The McMillans would have been most likely to take up the mantle for the restoration of children's centres, while Owen would have been most likely to engage in the curriculum debate.

Grace Owen states in her 1920 book *Nursery School Education*:

> The fostering of the creative impulses means the fostering of life itself… It is the great responsibility of the Nursery School to provide [the child] with the means and opportunity to express fully his own ideas and feelings… Careless gaiety and bubbling fun are true evidence of the untrammelled spirit, and where these are usually absent there is something wrong… some pressure from the grown-up helpers that needs to be removed, or some lack of unselfish sympathy.[83]

When asked about her philosophy of nursery education in BBC radio broadcast of 1923, Margaret McMillan said:

> You may ask, why should we give all this to the children? Because this is nurture, and without it they can never really have education… the educational system should grow out of the nursery schools system, not out of a neglected infancy… [in the nursery school] everything is planned for life…. If Great Britain will go forward [with open air nursery schools]… she will sweep away the cause of untold suffering, ignorance, waste and failure.[84]

These Grande Dames who engaged in pitched battle over the shaping of British Early Years education and care a century ago still have so much wisdom to offer policy makers today, if only they would listen.

REFLECTIVE QUESTIONS

- I have suggested above that the ideas and practice of the pioneers of modern Early Years education and care are still relevant today. Can you relate this to your own practice, and if so, how?
- Why do you think Eliot came down so firmly on Owen's 'side'? Do you agree with her? Or do you find her descriptions and judgements of McMillan unsympathetic?
- Would you be able to adopt the practice and ethos that McMillan and Owen pioneered into your practice? If not, how would you define the barriers? How could they be removed?
- Do you think that there are some practices advocated by McMillan and Owen that are not relevant or useful today, and if so, why?

END NOTES

1. Read, J. The Froebel movement in Britain 1900–1939.
2. Sims-Shouten, W. (2020) Victorian attitudes can still be found in child protection services today. *The Conversation Online.* Available at: https://theconversation.com/victorian-attitudes-can-still-be-found-in-child-protection-services-today-129510
3. Gilliard, D. (1998) Education in England, the history of our schools. Available at http://www.education england.org.uk/history/chapter06.html#02
4. Carter, P. and Thompson, K. (2005) 'Poverty', OU A825 block 6 readings. Source: Chapter 8 in Paul Carter and Kate Thompson, Sources for Local Historians (pp. 86, pp. 46–101, 209–11. Chichester: Phillimore).
5. Livesey, R. (2004) Reading for character: Women social reformers and narratives of the urban poor in late Victorian and Edwardian London. *Journal of Victorian Culture*, 9(1), 43–68, p. 50.
6. Livesey, p. 55.
7. McMillan, M. (1927) Life of Rachel McMillan (pp. 28–29). London: J.M. Dent.
8. Bradburn, E. and McMillan, M. (1976) Framework and Expansion of Nursery Education (p. 32). Redhill: Denholm House.
9. McMillan, M. Life of Rachel McMillan (p. 29).
10. McMillan, M. Life of Rachel McMillan (p. 81).
11. DuCharme, C., McMillan, M. and Montessori, M. (1992) Champions of the poor. Paper presented at the Annual Meeting of the National Association for the Education of Young Children (New Orleans, LA, November 12–15). Available at: https://files.eric.ed.gov/fulltext/ED368463.pdf
12. Celia Lascarides, V. and Hinitz, B.F. (2000) The first school baths in Britain were opened at the Wapping School in Bradford in 1897. History of early childhood education (p. 120). Abingdon: Routledge.
13. Welshman, J. (1997) School meals and milk in England and Wales, 1906–1945. *Medical History*, 41, 6–29.
14. Steedman, C. (1990) Childhood, culture and class in Britain: Margaret McMillan 1860–1931 (p. 49). New Jersey: Rutgers University Press.
15. The Fight for the Schools. The Yorkshire daily observer, 22nd September 1902, quoted in Bradbury, p. 63.
16. Yeo, S. (1977) A new life: The religion of socialism in Britain. History Workshop No 4 5–56 (p. 45).
17. McMillan, M. Life of Rachel McMillan (p. 115).

18. McMillan, M. Life of Rachel McMillan (p. 120).

19. University of Greenwich A94/16/A8/34: script of a programme broadcast by the BBC Home Service 27th November 1960. The source for the quote appears to have been Emma Stevinson, the first Principal of the Rachel McMillan Teacher Training College, who died in 1959.

20. McMillan, M. (1917) The Camp School (pp. 84–85). London: George Allen and Unwin.

21. Bradburn, p. 130.

22. Stevinson, E. and McMillan, M. (1954) Prophet and Pioneer (p. 8). London: University of London Press.

23. McMillan, M. (1917) The Camp School (p. 51). London: George Allen and Unwin.

24. McMillan, M. Life of Rachel McMillan (p. 186).

25. University of Greenwich A94/16/A1/86: letter from Margaret McMillan to 'Mr Mackenzie', 7th July 1930.

26. Lewisham Local History Library A94/6/1/69: letter from Stanley Baldwin to Margaret McMillan, 20th December 1928.

27. Elizabeth Ross, E. (1983) Survival networks: Women's neighbourhood sharing in London before World War I. History Workshop 15, 4–27 (p. 20).

28. Board of Education (England) Education Act 1921, 11 & 12 Geo. 5. c. 51. Available at: http://www.education england.org.uk/documents/acts/1921-education-act.htmll

29. Moriarty, V. and McMillan, M. (1998) I learn, to succor the helpless (p. 60). Nottingham: Educational Heretics Press.

30. Read, J. (2011) The Froebel movement in Britain 1900–1939 (p. 165). Unpublished PhD thesis. University of Roehampton.

31. Rebecca S. N. and Cochran, M. (2007) Early childhood education: An International Encyclopaedia (pp. 576–577). Westport CT: Praegar.

32. LSE BAECE 23/2: Pamphlet relating to the Mather and Shakespeare Street Nursery, 1920–1972.

33. Read, J. The Froebel movement in Britain (p. 16).

34. Brock, A., Jarvis, P. and Olusoga, Y. (2014) Perspectives on play: Learning for Life (2nd edn., p. 17). Abingdon: Routledge.

35. Celia Lascarides, V. and Hinitz, B.F. (2011) History of early childhood education (2nd edn., p. 118). London: Routledge.

36. Read, J. The Froebel movement in Britain 1900–1939 (p. 61).

37. LSE BAECE 23/2: Pamphlet relating to the Mather and Shakespeare Street Nursery, 1920–1972.

38. Jarvis, P. and Liebovich, B. (2015) British nurseries, head and heart: McMillan, Owen and the genesis of the education/care dichotomy. Women's History Review, 24(6), 917–937. Available at: http://www.tandfonline.com/ doi/pdf/10.1080/09612025.2015.1025662. http://dx.doi.org/10.1080/09612025.2015.1025662

39. Adams Eliot, A. Dictionary of Unitarian and Universalist Biography, ND. Available at: https://uudb.org/articles/ abigailadamseliot.html

40. Eliot, A. Director of the *Eliot-Pearson department of child study at Tufts University* http://www.concordlibrary. org/scollect/Fin_Aids/OH_Texts/eliot.html; she died in 1992, aged 100 http://www.nytimes.com/1992/11/02/us/ abigail-adams-eliot-100-dies-expert-in-nursery-school-training.html

41. Radcliffe Library, Schlesinger Institute MC327/20, Family and Personal Papers of Abigail Adams Eliot, 1921.

42. Radcliffe Library, Schlesinger Institute MC327/23, Family and Personal Papers of Abigail Adams Eliot, 1921.

43. Radcliffe Library, Schlesinger Institute MC327/23, Family and Personal Papers of Abigail Adams Eliot, 1921.

44. Radcliffe Library, Schlesinger Institute MC327/20, Family and Personal Papers of Abigail Adams Eliot, 1921.

45. Radcliffe Library, Schlesinger Institute MC327/20, Family and Personal Papers of Abigail Adams Eliot, 1921.

46. Radcliffe Library, Schlesinger Institute MC327/20, Family and Personal Papers of Abigail Adams Eliot, 1921.

47. Radcliffe Library, Schlesinger Institute MC327/23, Family and Personal Papers of Abigail Adams Eliot, 1921.

48. University of Greenwich A94/16/A8/19: letter written by Abigail Adams Eliot, Brooks School, Concord, MA, USA, ND.

49. Radcliffe Library, Schlesinger Institute MC327/23, Family and Personal Papers of Abigail Adams Eliot, 1921.

50. Radcliffe Library, Schlesinger Institute MC327/23, Family and Personal Papers of Abigail Adams Eliot, 1921.
51. University of Greenwich A94/16/A8/19: letter from Miss Abigail Eliot, Brooks School, Concord, MA, USA, ND, but in response to a call for memories of Margaret McMillan in her centenary year, 1960.
52. NSA (1925) Summary of meeting of the Nursery School Association, Saturday 3rd January 1925.
53. All underlined in original.
54. University of Greenwich A94/16/A1/74: letter from Margaret McMillan to Robert Blatchford 20th February 1929.
55. Lewisham Local History Library A94/2/10A: handwritten A4 sheet by Margaret McMillan, no title, ND, appears to be a fragment from a draft article, refers to 'now in 1924'.
56. McMillan, M. (1919) The nursery school (p. 109). London: J.M. Dent and Sons.
57. LSE BAECE 13/5 Ward, H. (1925) Official letter written to Grace Owen by member of the Board of Education.
58. LSE BAECE 13/5, Summary of meeting of the Nursery School Association, Saturday 3rd January 1925.
59. LSE BAECE 24/1, Statement of Policy from the Nursery School Association, 1925.
60. LSE BAECE 24/1, Bulletin of the Nursery School Association dated 1927.
61. LSE BAECE 24/1, note in Grace Owen's handwriting, ND.
62. LSE BAECE 13/6, letter dated 11th February 1929 from Shena D. Simon to Grace Owen.
63. LSE BAECE 13/6, letter dated 12th February 1929 from Grace Owen to Shena D. Simon.
64. LSE BAECE 13/8, letter dated 16th April 1929 from Margaret McMillan to Grace Owen.
65. LSE BAECE 13/9, letter dated 7th May 1929 from the NSA to Margaret McMillan (no signature present).
66. LSE BAECE 13/9, letter dated 18th May 1929 from Margaret McMillan to the NSA.
67. LSE BAECE 13/8, letter dated 8th May 1929 from Margaret McMillan to Lillian de Lissa.
68. LSE BAECE 13/9, letter dated 18th May 1929 from Margaret McMillan to Lillian de Lissa.
69. LSE BAECE 13/8, Sheet entitled 'resignation of Miss McMillan' dated 21st June 1929.
70. LSE BAECE 13/9, letter from Margaret McMillan to Grace Owen, dated 20th June 1929.
71. LSE BAECE 13/8, Sheet entitled 'resignation of Miss McMillan' dated 20th June 1929.
72. Jarvis, P. and Liebovich, B. British nurseries, head and heart: McMillan, Owen and the genesis of the education/care dichotomy.
73. LSE BAECE 13/9, letter from Margaret McMillan to Grace Owen, dated 1st March 1930.
74. Read, J. The Froebel movement in Britain 1900–1939 (p. 48).
75. Jarvis, P. and Liebovich, B. (2015) British nurseries, head and heart: McMillan, Owen and the genesis of the education/care dichotomy'. Women's History Review. Available at: http://www.tandfonline.com/doi/abs/10.1080/09612025.2015.1025662?journalCode=rwhr20#.VUZripPff4U
76. LSE BAECE 24/1, Bulletin of the Nursery School Association, nd, but refers to a recently issued pamphlet in 1936.
77. Grover, C. (2005) The National childcare strategy: The social regulation of lone mothers as a gendered reserve army of labour. Capital & Class, 29(1), 63–90.
78. Department for Children, Schools and Families. (2007) The early years foundation stage. London: Department for Children, Schools and Families. Available at: https://dera.ioe.ac.uk/6413/7/statutory-framework_Redacted.pdf
79. Brown, G. (2006) Forward in 'Making a Brew'. Seacroft: Heads Together.
80. Toynbee, P. Closing children's centres is the very opposite of 'levelling up'. The Guardian Online, 27th August 2020. Available at: https://www.theguardian.com/commentisfree/2020/aug/27/closing-childrens-centres-opposite-levelling-up
81. Singh, M. The 2007–2008 financial crisis in review. Investopedia Online, 29th August 2021. Available at: https://www.investopedia.com/articles/economics/09/financial-crisis-review.asp
82. Gaunt, C. Row breaks out between critics of the revised early years curriculum and DfE. Nursery World Online, 22nd July 2020. Available at: https://www.nurseryworld.co.uk/news/article/row-breaks-out-between-critics-of-the-revised-early-years-curriculum-and-dfe
83. Owen, G. (1920) Nursery School Education. London: Methuen and Co.
84. Mansbridge, A. and McMillan, M. (1932) Prophet and Pioneer. London: J.M. Dent: outlines the full text of a broadcast given by MM on BBC radio, on 17th November 1927, pp. 104–106.

BIBLIOGRAPHY

A Collection of Women Writers (1912) The Montessori method. [Online] Available at: https://digital. library.upenn.edu/women/montessori/method/method.html [Accessed 1 December 2021].

Ainsworth, M.D.S. (1978) The Bowlby-Ainsworth attachment theory. *Behavioural and Brain Sciences*, 1(3), 436–438.

Aljabreen, A. (2020) Montessori, Waldorf, and Reggio Emilia: A comparative analysis of alternative models of early childhood education. *International Journal of Early Childhood*, 52, 337–353. https://doi.org/ 10.1007/s13158-020-00277-1

American Psychological Association (APA) (2021) Urie Bronfenbrenner Award for lifetime contribution to developmental psychology in the service of science and society. Available at: https://www.apadivi-sions.org/division-7/awards/bronfenbrenner?_ga=2.121646541.730223597.1632747580-56230896.162912 6674 [Accessed 27 September 2021].

Aubrey, K. and Riley, A. (2015) *Understanding and Using Educational Theories*. London: SAGE.

Baker, J. and Abernethy, B. (2003) From play to practice: A developmental framework for the acquisition of expertise in team sport. In: J. Starkes and K.A. Ericsson, *Expert Performance in Sports: Advances in Research on Sport Expertise* (pp. 89–113). Champaign, IL: Human Kinetics.

Ball, C. (2004) *Start Right: The Importance of Early Learning*. London: Royal Society of Arts.

Baugh, J. (2017) Meaning-less differences: Exposing fallacies and flaws in 'the word gap' hypothesis that conceal a dangerous 'language trap' for low-income American families and their children. *International Multilingual Research Journal*, 11(1), 39–51.

Biber, B. (1939) Nursery school as the beginning of education. *The Young Child in Education*, I, 2–5.

Biber, B. (1942) A dream for the nursery years. *Progressive Education*, I9, 243–250.

Biber, B. (1972) The 'whole child,' individuality and values in education. In J.R. Squire, *A new look at Birth to Three: Supporting Our Youngest Children*. Learning and Teaching Scotland (2005). [online] Available at: http://www.oas.org/udse/readytolearn/BIRTH%20TO%20THREE.pdf [Accessed 1 January 2022].

Bloch, C. (2018) Working with the 10 principles of early childhood education: Revaluing stories and imagination for children's biliteracy learning in South Africa. In *The Routledge International Handbook of Froebel and Early Childhood Practice* (pp. 68–78). Abingdon: Routledge.

Borg, C. and Mayo, P. (2001) Social difference, cultural arbitrary and identity: An analysis of a new national curriculum document in a non-secular environment. *International Studies in Sociology of Education*, 11(1), 63–86.

Bourdieu, P. (1997a) *Les Trois États du Capital Culturel Actes de la recherche en sciences sociales* (pp. 3–6). Vol. 30. L'institution scolaire.

Bourdieu, P. (1997b) *Pascalian Meditations* (pp. 3–50). Stanford, CA: Standford University Press.

Bourdieu, P. and Passeron, J.J. (1977a) *Reproduction*. Translated from French by Richard Nice (1990). London: SAGE. Available at: https://monoskop.org/images/8/82/Bourdieu_Pierre_Passeron_Jean_Claude_Reproduction_in_Education_Society_and_Culture_1990.pdf [Accessed 23 July 2020].

Bourdieu, P. and Passeron, I.-C. (1977b) *Reproduction in Education, Sociely and Culture*. London: SAGE, 254 p. (Translated from: La reproduction: éMmentspour une théorie du systeme d'enseignement. Paris, France: Editions de Minuit, 1970. 279 p.) [Center for European Sociology, Paris, France].

Bowlby, J. (1979) The Bowlby-Ainsworth attachment theory. *Behavioral and Brain Sciences*, 2(4), 637–638.

Bowlby, J., Robertson, J. and Rosenbluth, D. (1952) A two-year-old goes to hospital. *The Psychoanalytic Study of the Child*, 7(1), 82–94.

Bradbury, A. (2021a) Early childhood pioneers: Keeping Bronfenbrenner at the heart of early years practice. [online] Available at: https://kinderly.co.uk/2021/11/09/early-childhood-pioneers-keeping-bronfenbrenner-at-the-heart-of-early-years-practice/ [Accessed 1 January 2022].

Bradbury, A. (2021b) *Foreword. Early Years Foundation Stage*. London: Learning Matters.

Brendtro, L. (2006) The vision of Urie Bronfenbrenner: Adults who are crazy about kids. *Reclaiming Children and Youth*, 15(3), 162–166.

Brodal, P. (2004) *The Central Nervous System: Structure and Function* (3rd edn.). New York, NY: Oxford University Press.

Bronfenbrenner, U. (1977) Toward an experimental ecology of human development. *American Psychologist*, 32(7), 513–531.

Bronfenbrenner, U. (1979) *The Ecology of Human Development: Experiments by Nature and Design*. Boston, MA: Harvard University Press.

Bronfenbrenner, U. (1990) *Who Cares for Children* (pp. 27–40). UNESCO. Available at: https://eprints.lib.hokudai.ac.jp/dspace/bitstream/2115/25254/1/12_P27-40.pdf [Accessed 12 October 2021].

Bronfenbrenner, U. (1994) Ecological models of human development. In T. Husen and T. Postlethwaite, *International Encyclopedia of Education* (2nd edn., Vol. 3, pp. 1643–1647). Oxford: Pergamon Press.

Bronfenbrenner, U. (1995) Developmental ecology through space and time: A future perspective. In P. Moen, G. Elder and K. Luscher, *Examining Lives in Context: Perspectives on the Ecology of Human Development*. Washington, DC: American Psychological Association Press.

Bronfenbrenner, U. (1999) Environments in developmental perspective: Theoretical and operational models. In S. Friedman and T. Wachs, *Measuring Environment Across the Lifespan: Emerging Methods and Concepts*. Washington, DC: American Psychological Association Press.

Bronfenbrenner, U. (2005) *Making Human Beings Human: Bioecological Perspectives on Human Development*. Thousand Oaks, CA: SAGE Publications. (First published 1971).

Bronfenbrenner, U. and Ceci, S. (1994) Nature-nurture reconceptualized in developmental perspective: A bioecological model. *Psychological Review*, 101(4), 568–586.

Brown, C.P. (2020) Introducing the text and examining the emergence, maintenance and expansion of gaps, deficits and risks through early childhood policy. In: F. Nuxmalo, *Disrupting and Countering Deficits in Early Childhood*. New York, Abingdon: Routledge.

Bruce, T. (2015) *Friedrich Froebel From: The Routledge International Handbook of Philosophies and Theories of Early Childhood Education and Care Routledge*. The Routledge International Handbook of Philosophies and Theories of Early Childhood Education and Care. Available at: routledgehandbooks.com.

Bruce, T. (1987) *Early Childhood Education*. London: Hodder and Stoughton.

Bruce, T. (2001) *Learning Through Play: Babies, Toddlers and the Foundation Years*. London: Hodder & Stoughton.

Bruce, T. (2003) Seeing play for what it is: Parents and professional workers together. *International Journal of Early Years Education*, 2(1), 17–22.

Bruce, T. (2004) *Developing Learning in Early Childhood*. London: Paul Chapman.

Bruce, T. (2015) *Early Childhood Education* (5th edn.). London: Hodder Education.

Bruce, T. (Ed.) (2012) *Early Childhood Practice: Froebel Today*. London: SAGE Publications. https://www.doi.org/10.4135/9781446251287

Bruce, T. (Ed.) (2013) *Early Childhood: A Guide for Students*. London: SAGE Publications.

Bruce, T. and Dyke, J. (2017, May 15) EYFS best practice: learning from Froebel… nurture, family and community. *Nursery World Monday*. Available at: https://www.nurseryworld.co.uk/features/article/eyfs-best-practice-learning-from-froebel-nurture-family-and-community

Bruner, J. (1960) *The Process of Education*. Cambridge, MA: The President and Fellows of Harvard College.

Buchan, T. (2013) *The Social Child. Laying the Foundations of Relationships and Language*. Oxford: Routledge.

Callanan, M., et al. (2017) Study of early education and development: Good practice in early education. [online] Available at: CODC (Center on the Developing Child) (2012). Executive Function (InBrief). www.developingchild.harvard.edu [Accessed 1 January 2022].

Carr, M. (2006) Learning dispositions and key competencies: A new curriculum continuity across the sectors? *Early Childhood Folio*, 10, 21–27.

Ceci, S. (2005) Family champion, policy advisor, and friend, *Association for Psychological Science*. Available at: https://www.psychologicalscience.org/observer/in-appreciation-urie-bronfenbrenner [Accessed 27 September 2021].

Channel 4. (2018) Old people's home for 4 year olds: Series 1 episode 1 – all 4. [online] Available at: channel4.com [Accessed 1 January 2022].

Cheruvu, R. (2020) Disrupting standardised education through culturally sustaining pedagogies with young children. In F. Nuxmalo, *Disrupting and Countering Deficits in Early Childhood*. New York, NY; Abingdon. Routledge.

Chesworth, L. (2016) A funds of knowledge approach to examining play interests: Listening to children's and parents' perspectives. *International Journal of Early Years Education*, 24(3), 294–308.

Conkbayir, M. (2017) *Early Childhood and Neuroscience: Theory, Research and Implications for Practice*. London: Bloomsbury Academic.

Conkbayir, M. (2021) *Early Childhood and Neuroscience* (2nd edn.). London. Bloomsbury.

Copple, C. and Bredekamp, S. (2009) *Developmentally Appropriate Practice in Early Childhood Programs Serving Children From Birth Through Age 8* (3rd edn.). Washington, DC: National Association for the Education of Young Children.

Cottell, J. (2019) Over half of parents with young children feel lonely, with those on lowest incomes twice as likely to be affected. *Coram Family and Childcare press release 17/11/2019*. Available at: https://www.familyandchildcaretrust.org/over-half-parents-young-children-feel-lonely-those-lowest-incomes-twice-likely-be-affected [Accessed 12 October 2021].

Csikszentmihalyi, M. (1996) *Creativity: Flow and the Psychology of Discovery and Invention*. New York, NY: HarperCollins.

Daniel, V. (2019) *Perceptions of a Leadership Crisis in the Early Years Sector (EYS)*. University of Birmingham. Ed.D. [online] Available at: https://etheses.bham.ac.uk/id/eprint/8787/ [Accessed 1 December 2021].

Daniel, V. (2021) Reframing safe spaces. *LGBTQIA Early Years Magazine*. Edited by Bradbury, A, p. 16.

Darling, N. (2007) Ecological systems theory: The person in the center of the circles. *Research in Human Development*, 4(3–4), 203–217.

Della Porta, S. (2021). In T. Bruce, L. McNair and J. Whinnett, *Putting Storytelling at the Heart of Early Childhood Practice: A Reflective Guide for Early Years Practitioners*. Journal of Early Childhood Literacy. https://doi.org/10.1177/14687984211046645

Demie, F. (2018) Raising achievement of black Caribbean pupils: Good practice for developing leadership capacity and workforce diversity in schools. *School Leadership and Management*, 39.

Department for Education (DfE) (2021) Statutory framework for the early years foundation stage: Setting the standards for learning, development and care for children from birth to five. Available at: www.dfe.gov.uk

Department of Education and Science (1988) *Education Reform Act: Local Management of Schools: Circular 7/88*. London: HMSO.

Department of Education and Science (1989) *National Curriculum: From Policy to Practice*. London: HMSO.

Dewey, J. (1933) *How We Think: A Restatement of the Relation of Reflective Thinking to the Educative Process*. Boston, MA: D.C. Heath & Co Publishers.

Dewey, J. (1938) *Experience and Education*. New York, NY: Macmillan.

DfE (2015) Pedagogy in early childhood education and care (ECEC): An international comparative study of approaches and policies. [online] Available at: publishing.service.gov.uk [Accessed 1 December 2021].

DfE (2021) Early years foundation stage. [online] Available at: https://www.gov.uk/government/publica-tions/changes-to-the-early-years-foundation-stage-eyfs-framework/changes-to-the-early-years-founda-tion-stage-eyfs-framework [Accessed 1 November 2021].

Doherty, J. and Hughes, M. (2009) *Child Development: Theory and Practice 0–11*. Harlow: Pearson.

Dudley-Marling, C. (2020) Rejecting deficit views of children in poverty in favour of a philosophy of abundance. In F. Nuxmalo, *Disrupting and Countering Deficits in Early Childhood*. New York, NY, Abingdon: Routledge.

Early Years Reviews (2020) Equality and diversity in the early years. [online] Available at: https://ear-lyyearsreviews.co.uk/product/equality-and-diversity-in-the-early-years/ [Accessed 11 December 2021].

Education Scot. Play Pedagogy. [online] Available at: education.gov.scot; https://education.gov.scot/improvement/Documents/sac86-play-pedagogy.pdf [Accessed 1 January 2022].

Erikson, E.H. (1963) *Childhood and Society* (2nd edn.). New York, NY: Norton.

Evans, E. and Price, M. (2012) Children and young people's social and emotional development. In N. Edmond and M. Price, *Integrated Working With Children and Young People*. London: SAGE.

Famm (2021) The Montessori method. [Online] Available at: https://www.fundacionmontessori.org/the-montessori-method.htm [Accessed 1 December 2021].

Figueroa Ofsted Lecture https://zoom.us/rec/play/FKEW6UOZWvyaI0wIeO0Taha1FEFEDPmqSWw70n7-0di2hbEV1klHApxwC1Dv0BfY4BgoWwjXiuH3e_wi.MoCsruCOGj5sO9hR [Accessed 26 January 2022].

Fisher, J. (1996) *Starting From the Child*. London: Open University Press.

Fisher, J. (2016) *Interacting or Interfering*. London: Open University Press.

Fisher, J. (2020a) *Moving on to Key Stage One* (2nd edn.). London: Open University Press.

Fisher, J. (2020b) *Moving on to Key Stage 1: Improving Transition into Primary School* (2nd edn.). Maidenhead: Open University Press.

Forest School Association. [online] Available at: https://forestschoolassociation.org [Accessed 1 January 2022].

Fowler, B. (2000) *Reading Bourdieu on Society and Culture*. Oxford. Blackwell.

Freire, P. (2000) *Pedagogy of Freedom*. Translated by P. Clark. New York, NY; Oxford: Rowman and Littlefield.

Freire, P. (1970) (1993 reprint) *Pedagogy of the Opressed*. London: Penguin Random House.

Freire, P. (2005) *The Pedagogy of the Oppressed*. New York, NY: Continuum.

Froebel Trust Website. [online] Available at: Froebel Trust | Homepage. [Accessed 1 January 2022].

Gardner, H. (1982) *Art, Mind, and Brain: A Cognitive Approach to Creativity*. New York, NY: Basic Books.

Giroux, H. (2011) *On Critical Pedagogy* (p. 8). New York, NY; London: Continuum Publishing.

Goleman, D. (1996) *Emotional Intelligence: Why It Can Matter More Than IQ*. London: Bloomsbury.

Gooch, K. (2010) *Towards Excellence in Early Years Education*. London. Routledge.

Goswami, U. (2006) Neuroscience and education: From research to practice? *Journal of Nature Review Neuroscience*, 7(5), 406–411.

Gov.UK (2015) *Study of early education and development (SEED)*. Department of Education. [online] Available at: https://www.gov.uk/government/collections/study-of-early-education-and-development-seed [Accessed 1 January 2022].

Gov.UK (2017) *Study of Early Education and Development (SEED)* [online] Available at: https://www.gov.uk/government/collections/study-of-early-education-and-development-seed [Accessed 1 January 2022].

Gov.UK (2019) *EYFSP Main Test*. Department for Education. [online] Available at: https://assets.publishing.service.gov.uk/government/uploads/system/uploads/attachment_data/file/839934/EYFSP_2019_Main_Text_Oct.pdf [Accessed 1 January 2022].

Gov.UK (2020) *Study of Early Education and Development (SEED): Impact Study on Early Education Use and Child Outcomes up to age five years Research report*. Department for Education. [online] Available at: https://assets.publishing.service.gov.uk/government/uploads/system/uploads/attachment_data/file/867140/SEED_AGE_5_REPORT_FEB.pdf [Accessed 1 January 2022].

Gray, C. and Macblain, S. (2015) *Learning Theories in Childhood* (2nd edn.). London: SAGE.

Gray, S.L. (2007) Teacher as technician: Semi-professionalism after the 1988 education reform act and its effect on conceptions of pupil identity. *Policy Futures in Education*, 5(2), 194–203. https://doi.org/10.2304/pfie.2007.5.2.194

Grenfell, M. (2006) Bourdieu in the field: From the Béarn and to Algeria – a timely response. *French Cultural Studies*, 17, 223–239.

Grenfell, M. (2008) *Pierre Bourdieu: Key Concepts* (p. 440). Durham: Acumen.

Grenfell, M. (2009) *Social capital in action: The case of partnership and network project in South of England*. University of Dublin, Educational Papers No. 1.

Grimmer, T. (2020) 10 Top tips for developing a 'loving pedagogy' in the early years. [online] Available at: https://kinderly.co.uk/2020/08/18/10-top-tips-for-developing-a-loving-pedagogy-in-early-years/ [Accessed 1 January 2022].

Grimmer, T. (2021) *Developing a Loving Pedagogy in the Early Years: How Love Fits with Professional Practice*. London: Routledge.

Hart, B. and Risley, T. (1995) *Meaningful Differences in the Everyday Experience of Young American Children*. Baltimore, MD; London; Sydney, NSW: Paul Brookes Publishing.

Hayes, N., O'Toole, L. and Halpenny, A. (2017) *Introducing Bronfenbrenner: A Guide for Practitioners and Students in Early Years Education*. London: Routledge.

Hedges, H., Cullen, J. and Jordan, B. (2011) Early years curriculum: Funds of knowledge as a conceptual framework for children's interests. *Journal of Curriculum Studies*, 43(2), 185–205.

Henry-Allain, L. and Lloyd Rose, M. (2021) *The tiney Guide to Being an Antiracist Early Educator*. Tiney. [online]Available at: https://assets.ctfassets.net/jnn9p19md0ig/4ntGEh21KNXyB9aLxq9gCY/61847fa97f563ba4d9b281cf89d8a8ef/Guide_Inclusive_Education.pdf [Accessed 4 March 2022].

Hirsh-Pasek, K., Golinkoff, R.M., Berk, L.E. and Singer, D.G. (2008) *A Mandate for Playful Learning in Preschool: Presenting the Evidence*. New York, NY: Oxford University Press.

Hirsh-Pasek, K., Golinkoff, R., Berk, L. and Singer, D. (2009) *A Mandate for Playful Learning in Preschool. Reading the Evidence* (p. 2). New York, Oxford. Oxford University Press.

Hodgeman, L. (2012) *Enabling Environments in the Early Years. Making Provision*. London. Andrews UK.

Howard, J. and McInnes, J. (2012) The impact of children's perceptions of an activity as play rather than not play on emotional wellbeing. *Child: Care, Health and Development*, 29(5), 737–742.

https://assets.publishing.service.gov.uk/government/uploads/system/uploads/attachment_data/file/839934/EYFSP_2019_Main_Text_Oct.pdf [Accessed 03 August 2021].

OMEP. (2020) Towards a democratic early childhood education for all. Moss. P,. [online] Available at: https://omepworld.org/towards-a-democratic-early-childhood-education-for-all-peter-moss/ [Accessed 1 January 2022].

Hunter, B., Renfrew, M. J., Downe, S., Royal College of Midwives, Cheyne, H., Dykes, F., Lavender, T., Page, L., Sandall, J., and Spiby, H. (2020, May 19) *Supporting the Emotional Wellbeing of Midwives in a Pandemic: Guidance for RCM*. Royal College of Midwives. Available at: https://www.rcm.org.uk/media/4095/rcm-supporting-the-emotional-wellbeing-of-midwives-during-a-pandemic-v1-submitted-to-rcm_mrd.pdf

ICAN. Talking About a Generation - A Review Into Current Policy, Evidence and Practice for Speech, Language and Communication. [online] Available at: https://ican.org.uk/i-cans-talking-point/professionals/tct-resources/more-resources/talking-about-a-generation/ [Accessed 1 January 2022].

Jarvis, P., et al. (2017) *Early Years Pioneers in Context: Their Lives, Lasting Influence, and Impact on Practice Today*. London: Routledge.

Johnson, E.J. (2015) Debunking the 'language gap'. *Journal for Multicultural Education*, 9(1), 42–50.

Karst, P. (2018) *The Invisible String*. New York, NY: Little, Brown and Company.

King, A. (1993, Winter) From sage on the stage to guide on the side. *College Teaching*, 41(1), 30–35.

Laevers, F. (2000) Forward to basics! Deep-level-learning and the experiential approach. *Early Years*, 20(2), 20–29. https://doi.org/10.1080/0957514000200203

Lane, J. (2007, Spring) Culture, ethnicity, language, faith and equal respect in early childhood – does 'getting it' matter? *Education Review*, 20(1), 101–107.

Legislation.gov.uk (2010) Equality act 2010. [online] Available at: http://www.legislation.gov.uk/ukpga/2010/15/contents [Accessed 1 January 2022].

Lego Foundation (2017) Learning through play: A review of the evidence. [online] Available at: https://www.legofoundation.com/media/1063/learning-through-play_web.pdf [Accessed 1 January 2022].

Lego Foundation (2021) The neuroscience of learning through Play. [online] Available at: https://learningthroughplay.com/explore-the-research/the-neuroscience-of-learning-through-play/ [Accessed 1 December 2021].

Lillard, A. (2008) How important are the Montessori materials. [online] Available at: https://www.montessorisociety.org.uk/Articles/4441937 [Accessed 1 December 2021].

Lundahl, L., Erixon, A.I. and Holm, A.S. (2013) Marketization of education in Sweden: How far has it gone? *Education Inquiry*, 4(3), 97–514.

Malaguzzi, L. (1994) Your image of the child: Where teaching begins. *Early Childhood Educational Exchange*, 96, 52–61.

Malaguzzi, L. (1998) *History, ideas, and basic philosophy: An interview with Lella Gandini*. In The hundred languages of children: The Reggio Emilia approach—advanced reflections, Edited by: Edwards, C., Gandini, L. and Forman, G. 49–97. Westport, CT.

Manning, J.P. (2005) Rediscovering Froebel: A call to re-examine his life & gifts. *Early Childhood Education Journal*, 32(6), 371–376. https://doi.org/10.1007/s10643-005-0004-8

Mardell, B., Lynneth Solis, S. and Bray, O. (2019) The state of play in school: Defining and promoting playful learning in formal education settings, *International Journal of Play*, 8(3), 232–236.

Marek, W. (2019) Heritage interpretation through an architectural design. *SHS Web of Conferences, 64.* DOI: 10.1051/shsconf/20196403009

Marshall, C. (2017) Montessori education: A review of the evidence base. *npj Science of Learning*, 2, 11. https://doi.org/10.1038/s41539-017-0012-7

Maslow, A. (1970) *Motivation and Personality* (2nd edn.). New York, NY: Harper and Row.

McClelland, M.M., et al. (2012) Relations between pre-school attention span-persistence at age 25 educational outcomes, *Early Childhood Research Quarterly*, 28, 314–324. NFER (2005) National Foundation for Educational research study of transition from the foundation stage to key stage 1.

Merton, R.K. (1968) The Matthew effect in science. *Science*, 159(3810), 56–63. Bibcode:1968Sci...159...56M. https://doi.org/10.1126/science.159.3810.56. PMID 17737466. S2CID 3526819.

Montessori Society. [online] Available at: Montessori Society AMI (UK) – Home. [Accessed 1 January 2022].

Montessori, M. (1913) *Pedagogical Anthropology (New York 1913)* (pp. 17–98). Quoted in Kramer.

Moss, D. (2019) *Democracy. A Case Study*. London. Belknap Press.

Moss, P. (2020) *Towards a democratic early childhood education for all available*. World Organisation for Early Education. [online] Available at: https://omepworld.org/towards-a-democratic-early-childhood-education-for-all-peter-moss [Accessed 1 January 2022].

Moyles, J. and Yates, R. (2004) Effective leadership and management evaluation scheme (early years). *Report on a Research Project Sponsored by Essex County Council: The Schools Service, Southend Borough Council and the European Social Fund*. Chelmsford: Anglia Polytechnic University/Essex County Council.

Nimmo, J. and Park, S. (2009) Engaging Early Childhood Teachers in the Thinking and Practice of Inquiry: Collaborative Research Mentorship as a Tool for Shifting Teacher Identity. *Journal of Early Childhood Teacher Education*, 30(1), 93–104.

Nurturing Parenting *Stephen J. Bavolek PhD, Principle Author of the Nurturing Parenting Programs, Assessments, and Founder of Family Development Resources, Inc* (Est. 1983). [online] Available at: https://www.nurturingparenting.com [Accessed 1 January 2022].

O'Connor, A. (2013) *Understanding Transitions in Early Years*, Abingdon: Routledge.

Ofsted (2014) Are you ready? [online] Available at: https://assets.publishing.service.gov.uk/government/uploads/system/uploads/attachment_data/file/418819/Are_you_ready_Good_practice_in_school_readiness.pdf [Accessed 1 December 2021].

Ofsted (2017) Bold beginnings. Available at: https://assets.publishing.service.gov.uk/government/uploads/system/uploads/attachment_data/file/663560/28933_Ofsted_-_Early_Years_Curriculum_eport_-_Accessible.pdf [Accessed 29 October 2021].

Ofsted (2021) School inspection handbook. [online] Available at: https://www.gov.uk/government/publications/school-inspection-handbook-eif/school-inspection-handbook [Accessed 1 January 2022].

Ornstein, P.A., Haden, C.A. and San Souci, P. (2010) The development of skilled remembering in children. In: J.H. Byrne and H. Roediger III, *Learning and Memory: A Comprehensive Reference: Volume 4, Cognitive Psychology of Memory*. Kidlington; Oxford: Elsevier.

Papadopoulou, M. (2012) The ecology of role play: Intentionality and cultural evolution. *British Educational Research Journal*, 38(4), 575–592.

Pascal, P. and Bertram, T. (2016) High achieving white working class boys project. *Centre for Research in Early Childhood*. Available at: http://www.crec.co.uk/hawwc-boys [Accessed 08 May 2020].

Piaget, J. (1959) *The Language and Thought of the Child* (Vol. 5). London: Psychology Press.

Piaget, J. (1973) *The Child and Reality: Problems of Genetic Psychology* (Translated by A. Rosin). Grossman: Oxford.

Plomin, R. and Bergeman, C. (1991) The nature of nurture: Genetic influence on 'environmental' measures. *Behavioral and Brain Sciences*, 14, 373–427.

Pound, L. (2011) *Influencing Early Childhood Education. Key Figures, Philosophies and Ideas*. Maidenhead: Open University Press.

Pritchard, A. (2018) *Ways of Learning: Learning Theories for the Classroom*. Abingdon: Routledge.

Progressive education (1972). ASCD Yearbook. Washington, DC: Association for Supervision and Curriculum Development.

Ramsey, D. (2014) *The Play Deficit Disorder Crisis*. Scotts Valley, CA: Create Space Publishing.

Reed-Danahay, D. (2005) *Locating Bourdieu* (pp. 46–47). Bloomington, IN: Indiana University Press.

Robbins, D. (1991) *The Work of Pierre Bourdieu* (p. 2). Buckingham: Open University Press.

Robbins, D. (2000) *Bourdieu and culture*. London: Sage.

Rosa, E. and Tudge, J. (2013) Urie Bronfenbrenner's theory of human development: Its evolution from ecology to bioecology. *Journal of Family Theory & Review*, 5(4), 243–258.

Sahlberg, P. and Doyle, W. (2020) *Let the Children Play: For the Learning, Well-Being, and Life Success of Every Child*. Oxford: Oxford University Press.

Salamanca Statement. [online] Available at: www.right-to-education.org/sites/right-to-education.org/files/resource-attachments/Salamanca_Statement_1994.pdf [Accessed 1 December 2021].

Schlieber, M. and Mclean, C. (2020) Educator work environments are children's learning environments: How and why they should be improved. *Center for the Study of Child Care Employment*. Available at: https://cscce.berkeley.edu/educator-work-environments-are-childrens-learning-environments-how-and-why-they-should-be-improved/

Seden, J. (2006) Frameworks and theories. In J. Aldgate, D. Jones, W. Rose and C. Jeffery, *The Developing World of the Child*. London: Jessica Kingsley Publishers.

Servos, J., Dewar, B., Bosack S. & Coplan, R. (2016) Canadian early childhood educators' perceptions of young children's gender-role play and cultural identity. *Journal of Early Childhood Research*, 14(3), 324–332.

Shonkoff, J.P. and Phillips, D.A. (eds) (2000) *From Neurons to Neighborhoods: The Science of Early Childhood Development*. Washington, DC: National Academy Press.

Siraj Blatchford, I. and Sylva, K. (2002) *Researching Effective Pedagogy in the Early Years*, London: Institute of Education.

Skolnick-Weisberg, D., Kittredge, A., Hirsh-Pasek, K., Golinkoff, R. and Khlar, D. (2015) Making play work for education: Research demonstrates that guided play can help preschool children prepare for reading and math better than free play and direct instruction alone. *Phi Delta Kappan*, 96(8).

Sriram, R. (2020) Why ages 2–7 matter so much for brain development. [online] Available at: https://www.edutopia.org/article/why-ages-2-7-matter-so-much-brain-development?fbclid=IwAR1M1sxQMEsPZybeDt0rXqaPEOdwTp3HY-kq4uLIsYUjWJbuWonH1W830Xc [Accessed 1 January 2022].

Stewart, N. (2011) *How Children Learn*. London: British Association for Early Childhood.

Sylva, K., Melhuish, E., Sammons, P., Siraj-Blatchford, I. and Taggart, B. (2004) The Effective Provision of Pre-School Education (EPPE) Project: Findings from Pre-school to End of Key Stage 1. By *Institute of Education, University of London, +University of Oxford, #Birkbeck, University of London, ~University of Nottingham.

The Early Years Coalition (2021) Birth to five matters: Non statutory guidance for the early years foundation stage. Available at: https://birthto5matters.org.uk/download-or-buy-a-copy/ [Accessed 1 December 2021].

The Hundred Languages of Children: The Reggio Emilia Approach (1998) (p. 83). Greenwich: Ablex Publishing.

Thomas, F. and Harding, S. (2011) The role of play: The outdoors as the medium and mechanism for well-being, learning and development. In J. White, *Outdoor Provision in the Early Years*. London: SAGE Publications.

Tickell, C. (2011) *The Early Years: Foundations for Life, Health and Learning*. London: An Independent Report on the Early Years Foundation Stage to Her Majesty's Government.

Tudge, J., Mokrova, I., Hatfield, B. and Karnik, R. (2009) Uses and misuses of Bronfenfrenner's bio-ecological theory of human development. *Journal of Family Theory and Review*, 1(4), 198–210.

Tudge, J., Payir, A., Merçon-Vergas, E., Hongjian, C., Liang, Y., Li, J. and O'Brien, L. (2016) Still misused after all these years? A reevaluation of the uses of Bronfenbrenner's bioecological theory of human development. *Journal of Family Theory and Review*, 8(4), 427–445.

UNCRC Website. [online] Available at: UN convention on the rights of the child (UNCRC) – UNICEF UK [Accessed 1 December 2021].

Vermes, S. (2008) What are the features of the adult's contributions which create good interactions during child-initiated activity. Unpublished dissertation. Oxford Brooks University (quoted in Moving on to Key Stage One).

Vygotsky, L.S. (1978) *Mind in Society: The Development of Higher Psychological Processes*. Cambridge, MA: Harvard University Press.

Vygotsky, L.S. (1934) *The Collected Works of L.S. Vygotsky, Vol. 1: Problems of General Psychology* (pp. 39–285). New York, NY: Plenum Press. (Original work published 1934.)

Webb, J., Schirato, T. and Danaher, G. (2002) *Understanding Bourdieu*. Crows Nest, NSW: Allen & Unwin.

Weisberg, D.S., Hirsh-Pasek, K. and Golinkoff, R.M. (2013) Guided play: Where curricular goals meet a playful pedagogy. *Mind, Brain, and Education*, 7(2), 104–112.

White, R., Prager, E.O., Schaefer, C., Kross, E., Duckworth, A.L. and Carlson, S.M. (2017) The 'Batman effect': Improving perseverance in young children. *Child Development*, 88(5), 1563–1571.

Whitebread, D. (2012a) *The Importance of Play*. Cambridge: University of Cambridge.

Whitebread, D. (2012b) *Developmental Psychology and Early Childhood Education*, London: SAGE.

Whitebread, D. (2014) The importance of self-regulation for learning from Birth. In H. Moylett, *The Characteristics of Effective Early Learning*. Maidenhead: Open University Press.

Whitebread, D. (2016, Autumn) Self-regulation in early childhood education. *Early Education Journal*, No. 80, 3.

Wilson, J.J. and Bavolek, S.J. (2000). *The Nurturing Parenting Programs*. [online] Available at: https://www.ncjrs.gov/pdffiles1/ojjdp/172848.pdf [Accessed 5 July 2020].

World Health Organization (2020). Improving early childhood provision. Available at: https://www.ncbi.nlm.nih.gov/books/NBK555073/pdf/Bookshelf_NBK555073.pdf

Wyse, D. and Torrance, H. (2009) The development and consequences of national curriculum assessment for primary education in England. *Educational Research*, 51(2), 213–228. https://doi.org/10.1080/00131880902891479

Yee, M. (2019) Why 'safe spaces' are important for mental health – especially on college campuses. [online] Available at: https://www.healthline.com/health/mental-health/safe-spaces-college#1 [Accessed 1 January 2022].

Zeedyk, S. (2012) Babies come into the world already connected to other people… Available at: http://www.suzannezeedyk.com/wp-content/uploads/2016/03/Suzanne-Zeedyk-Babies-Connected-v2.pdf

Zeedyk, S. (2013) *Sabre Tooth Tigers and Teddy Bears: The Connected Baby Guide to Understanding Attachment*. Dundee: Suzanne Zeedyk.

INDEX